NATURAL CAT CARE

NATURAL CAT CARE

ALTERNATIVE THERAPIES FOR CAT HEALTH AND VITALITY

A complete guide with over 280 practical photographs

John Hoare
BVSc MRCVS VetMFHom

Photography by Jane Burton

LORENZ BOOKS

This edition is published by Lorenz Books
an imprint of Anness Publishing Ltd
Blaby Road, Wigston
Leicestershire LE18 4SE
info@anness.com

www.lorenzbooks.com
www.annesspublishing.com

If you like the images in this book and would
like to investigate using them for publishing,
promotions or advertising, please visit our website
www.practicalpictures.com for more information.

A CIP catalogue record for this book
is available from the British Library.

Publisher: Joanna Lorenz
Project Editor: Sarah Ainley
Photographer: Jane Burton
Illustrator: Anna Koska
Copy Editor: Raje Airey
Cover Design: Nigel Partridge
Designer: Lisa Tai
Production Controller: Mai-Ling Collyer

ADDITIONAL PHOTOGRAPHY
t=top; b=bottom; l=left; r=right
John Daniels © Anness Publishing Limited p26t;
Michelle Garrett © Anness Publishing Limited p56t
and br, p57t; Kim Taylor p81t.

DISCLAIMER

This book is not intended to replace
advice from a qualified veterinary
practitioner. Physical illness – both acute
and chronic – nutritional difficulties and
environmental stresses can all cause
imbalances which may not respond to
appropriate natural therapies. Please
seek a professional opinion if you have
any doubts about your cat's health.
Neither the author nor the publisher
can accept any liability for failure
to follow this advice.

PUBLISHER'S NOTE

Although the advice and information in this book are
believed to be accurate and true at the time of going to
press, neither the authors nor the publisher can accept
any legal responsibility or liability for any errors or omissions
that may have been made nor for any inaccuracies nor for
any loss, harm or injury that comes about from following
instructions or advice in this book.

Contents

Introduction 6

section 1
Everyday Natural Cat Care 12

section 2
Holistic Therapies 30

An alternative view 32

Physical therapies 34

Medicinal therapies 46

Energy therapies 52

section 3
Holistic Cat Care 60

Treating your cat 62

Behavioural problems 64

Physical problems 71

First aid treatments 92

The death of your cat 94

Useful addresses 95

Index 96

Introduction

From ancient times it has been recognized that there

is an intimate relationship between the activity and

life of animals and their natural environment.

The Yellow Emperor's Classic of Medicine, 250BC

The philosophy of harmony and balance

Achieving harmony and balance is the goal of all natural healing therapies. All living organisms – whether human or animal – exist in an inter-dependent relationship with one another in nature. When this balance is disturbed, the result can lead to illness and disease.

conventional v holistic

Orthodox veterinary medicine is primarily concerned with treating physical symptoms of disease. Medical science is geared towards trying to understand in greater and greater detail how the physical body works, and there is now an incredible wealth of knowledge about the body's physical make-up and structure. This knowledge forms the basis of both human and animal medicine.

Science is reluctant to acknowledge the existence of things that cannot be measured. Because it is difficult to measure invisible emotional and psychological states, orthodox veterinary science largely ignores the effects of these when considering the health of an animal. Holistic medicine, on the other hand, whether for humans or animals, is not only concerned with the visible, physical body, but also with the intangible mental and emotional world of the patient. It maintains that true health is the harmony that is achieved when the mind, body and spirit are healthy and in a state of balance with one another.

Conventional scientific opinion is more prepared to accept those holistic therapies with a physical or medicinal basis than the invisible energy-based therapies, which often defy rational explanation.

accepting the theory

Energy therapies are based on the idea that the body contains a subtle energy system, radiating out as an aura. Imbalances in this system create disturbances which first show up on a mental and emotional level before they become physical reality and disease. There is some evidence to suggest that the body may be surrounded by such a system.

Kirlian photography demonstrates that the electromagnetic field of the body extends beyond its physical form. Some people believe this to be a reflection of the aura. Sequential images, taken during holistic sessions with human patients, show that the aura becomes more well-defined as the session progresses. Kirlian photographs taken of diseased and healthy parts of the body allow for a comparison of the auras, with diseased areas showing a weaker aura than healthy parts.

If we could measure the body's aura – to show when the body is working efficiently and alert us to imbalance and disease – magnetic vibrations could be fed back to the weak body, and a self-healing process could then be initiated.

defining health

Western culture usually defines health in terms of soundness of the mind and body, and disease as its opposite: an illness of the body and/or the mind. Health and disease are defined in terms of each other: good health is an absence of illness.

A holistic approach takes a different view. The distinction between health and disease is not so black and white, but is seen in terms of a continuum, with optimum health at one end of the scale and serious illness or even death at the other. Good health is regarded as a natural, balanced state of being, at one with the world and at ease. When this sublime state is broken, a state of dis-ease is created in which mental and physical abnormalities can develop.

natural lifestyle

For animals and humans alike, the move towards increasing levels of health and vitality involves taking into account the environmental and lifestyle factors.

When you take a cat into your home as a pet, you artificially restrict its interaction with nature and the world. This means that you become responsible for making sure your cat can lead a healthy life. A cat's basic needs are very similar to your own. It needs a good, clean place to live and the right sort of food to eat. It needs enough exercise to keep its body fit and healthy, and it needs protection from any form of prolonged or excessive stress. Most importantly, your cat needs to be treated in a kind and loving way. Emotional contentment is recognized universally as the one foundation for good health and resistance to disease. This book is designed to help you achieve that state for your cat.

◁ A healthy cat is happy and alert. It is active, curious about its surroundings and reacts to all stimuli quickly and appropriately.

△ In spite of all our efforts to domesticate it, the cat remains close to nature, and it enjoys the opportunity to walk by itself in open countryside. Cats have retained their natural hunting instinct and, in the absence of live prey, they will hunt suitable inanimate objects.

By devising hunting and chasing games to play around the home or garden, owners can make use of this natural instinct to promote bonding. Cats will also enjoy being stroked by humans they trust, provided that they do not feel their independence is compromised.

Good health in cats

Cats are graceful, elegant and independent animals and, treated correctly, they make wonderful pets. As mammals, their life cycle closely mirrors our own.

A new-born cat begins its life as a kitten, in which state it is totally dependent upon its mother. After a few weeks, it is weaned and begins to learn how to socialize and how to keep itself clean. This period is followed by a short adolescent stage, during which time social training is completed, and the young cat learns how to hunt for itself. Mature adulthood follows, and the cat becomes old and eventually dies. The average lifespan of a cat is 16 years.

A cat has the same basic requirements throughout its life. These will be influenced by its age and the type of lifestyle that it is allowed to lead. Kittens and young cats are more lively than older ones and need more opportunities for play and exercise. Consequently, a fit, active, young cat needs more food than an elderly one. Generally speaking, older cats are more sedentary, and may need special diets which cater for specific health conditions.

Cats are all more or less the same shape and size, regardless of their breeding group. Distinguishing features tend to be the length of fur, fur colour and patterning, and the shape, size and colour of the eyes.

△ Cats demonstrate their grace and elegance to the best effect as they explore their surroundings. Most cats will be happier if allowed the freedom to roam outdoors at will.

Whether pedigree or non-pedigree, and regardless of distinguishing features, fit, healthy cats share certain characteristics. Their coats are in good condition and do not smell. Their eyes are bright and their faces are alert and clean and are not stained by tear-spillage and other discharges. Their ears and nostrils are clean, without any discharge or smell. A healthy cat moves with ease and grace and does not limp. It is able to exercise under normal conditions, without coughing or showing signs of distress, for a period of time commensurate with its age. Like us, cats may tire more quickly as they grow older, but they should still move easily and without pain, and they should be able to enjoy all that life offers.

Conventional veterinary medicine is used to treat the physical symptoms of a sick animal. A holistic approach is appropriate for sick and well animals alike, and will encourage an optimum level of health for your pet. It looks at the animal as a whole, to prevent disease occurring. Providing your cat with a lifestyle suited to its daily physical and emotional needs forms part of the holistic approach, and will help to ensure that it lives a long and healthy life.

▷ The natural curiosity of the cat is displayed in young cats which hunt and play with more unusual objects found around the home.

Holistic medicine

The approach taken by the medical profession, and by veterinary specialists, is based on the scientific method of examining the world in order to understand it. A patient's symptoms are examined in minute detail, sometimes to the exclusion of everything else. Drugs are selected for the effect that they have on the system, organ or tissue that is thought to be causing the illness. The problems that the drugs may inadvertently cause in other parts of the body are accepted as inevitable side effects which have to be tolerated. All patients are treated in the same way and are expected to respond to treatment in a similar fashion, with little allowance made for individuality.

A holistic approach is more broadly based and endeavours to treat the patient (human or animal) and their unique needs, rather than the disease itself. Emotional, mental and physical characteristics all have a part to play in the development of illness and these are taken into account during treatment. One of the main difficulties in transferring a holistic approach from humans to animals is that an animal cannot tell you what it feels or thinks. If you are interested in complementary treatment for your cat, you need to pay close attention to its behaviour and notice any marked changes or mood swings. The vet and any

△ A quiet moment spent performing a simple massage on your cat can be beneficial when minor strains occur.

other practitioners involved will be relying on you in much the same way as a doctor treating a young child relies on its parents for information.

Sometimes, a course of treatment using only one method or therapy will not prove to be totally effective. In such a case, you or the vet

may suggest trying other approaches. It is important that the vet and other therapists involved in the case talk to each other and explain how their treatment works and how it interacts with any other treatment: aromatherapy can inhibit the action of homeopathic remedies, for example, while massage is compatible with all therapies.

The prime concern of any form of veterinary care is how it will affect the quality of the animal's life. The holistic approach does not ignore conventional science but tries to work alongside it. Natural forms of treatment can promote well-being in a healthy cat and can be used in order to alleviate the distress of illness, but if modern drugs are needed for chronic cases of disease then they should be given.

◁ The sensitivity of cats enables them to respond well to the gentle Bach Flower remedies.

◁ A sick cat will instinctively be attracted to the aromatherapy oil that can help it when unwell.

Everyday Natural Cat Care

Many times an illness begins when one is unaware of an imbalance that has subtly begun. Do not forget that the myriad things of the universe have an intimate relationship with one another.

*The Yellow Emperor's Classic of Medicine, 250*BC

Responsible cat ownership

Cats can be extremely good companions. They are sensitive, private creatures, and they do not need constant attention from their owners in order to be happy. They do not require much supervised exercise and, consequently, they are excellent pets for the elderly and for people with busy lives.

Although friendly and emotional by nature, cats are noted for being unfaithful. Many cats have two or more homes and may develop a routine where they spend part of each day with different people. It is not uncommon for a cat to breakfast at one house, lunch at a second and dine at a third; this can lead to obesity on what appears to be a normal diet. Nevertheless, if you are the cat's owner, it is always your responsibility to provide shelter, food and water for your pet.

should I have a cat?

Cats are relatively easy to look after and do not make great physical demands upon your time and energy. As with all pets, however, they need responsible owners.

Many people decide to keep a cat for companionship, but cats are independent creatures and may seem to take more than they give in return. They do show love and affection, but on their terms. In rural areas,

a cat can help to keep away rats and mice. In this case, find a kitten from a mother who is known to be a good hunter: she will have taught it well. If you have children, you may be thinking of having a pet as part of the family. The relationships children form with cats, as with all pets, teach them valuable emotional lessons about life, love, death and grief.

the cost of keeping a cat

In the household the cat will need a place of its own to rest and sleep, its own food and water, and a litter tray for hygiene purposes. If you want the cat to be house-trained, you will also need to make sure it can get in and out of the building easily. This may mean installing a cat flap.

While the financial outlay for cat equipment is low, the cost of the cat itself can vary from "free to a good home" to a substantial amount for a pedigree animal. Ongoing costs include feeding and vets' fees. You may decide to put your cat in a cattery when you go on holiday, which will add to the cost of the trip. A reputable cattery will insist that the cat has a valid certificate of vaccination. Vaccination is normally done when the cat is young and

the injections are repeated throughout its life with an annual booster. To take your cat abroad, you will need to follow the legal code of your own country and of any other country you plan to visit, and this will usually mean a rabies vaccination and microchipping. The microchip is a small silicon capsule that is implanted under the skin and contains information about the cat's identity: name and vaccination history, and the owner's name and address. The microchipping of pets is becoming popular, and is a helpful way of identifying animals lost or injured in road accidents.

Although cats are relatively easy to look after, some long-haired cats are difficult, if not impossible, to groom unless they are sedated or even anaesthetized. Vets' fees throughout the cat's life are likely to include vaccinations, neutering, and treatments for sickness and injury. Pet insurance is widely available, although there will often be a minimum charge if you make a claim.

The time commitment of keeping a cat is at its most demanding when kittens need house-training. Cats are naturally clean animals, however, and this is usually a short period. Adult cats will need at least two half-hour periods of playtime per day. If the cat is permanently housed indoors, it will need extensive play apparatus and plenty of attention to prevent boredom.

choosing the right cat

Kittens should be bought as soon as possible after weaning. Kittens learn to socialize between two and nine weeks, which means that the more contact they have with humans during this time, the friendlier they will become. Choose a kitten that is used to people and is comfortable with being handled. Rehoming adult cats can be more difficult as they are prone to return to their old home, and will wander off from their new territory; adult cats will settle in easier if they already know you.

▷ Children will often show a great empathy with young animals. While the children learn emotional lessons, the kittens learn to socialize with humans.

△ Taking care of your cat means providing it with the lifestyle that suits its needs. Ideally, cats should be allowed to roam freely outdoors. This ensures they get adequate exercise, and can satisfy their natural curiosity and develop their hunting instincts all at the same time.

In urban areas, if you live in an apartment, it may be safer to house your cat indoors permanently. In this case, you will need to provide plenty of opportunity for play. Cats become bored easily, and a lack of stimulation may encourage the onset of listlessness and ill health.

Housing your cat

Before you bring a new cat home, you need to decide where it will live, sleep and eat. Cats are normally allowed to live and sleep in the house, apart from stud-toms which are usually housed in special pens outside.

For reasons of good hygiene, it is not recommended that cats are allowed the freedom of the kitchen or bedroom. Dirty paw prints in food-preparation areas and fleas in the bedroom should be enough to convince most people that freedom of movement for the cat is not a good thing. Cats, however, are independent-minded creatures, and they will often try to assume forbidden privileges. You may need to keep doors and windows closed in order to make an area entirely cat-free. If a cat is to be housed indoors permanently, provision for suitable amounts of exercise must be made.

the cat's bed

A cat must have a bed of its own. Although wicker baskets look nice, they can be very difficult to clean if they become soiled. A simple, plastic basket, with or without a hood, is a good, practical choice. For

△ Soft beds are comfortable but they should be made from machine-washable materials. A removable "one way" liner improves comfort and hygiene.

warmth and comfort the basket needs to be lined with something such as an old jumper or a blanket. There are several proprietary materials available which allow fluids to pass through them whilst the top surface remains dry. These materials are machine-washable. An alternative to a basket is a padded hammock that hangs on a radiator. Many cats, especially elderly ones, like to be as warm as possible, and will often prefer these hammocks to ordinary baskets.

cat flaps

The provision of a cat flap is controversial. If your cat is allowed outside, having a flap enables it to come and go as it pleases. This means that the cat can be left to its own devices for long periods of time, which is useful if you are away from home often. However, a cat flap will also provide other cats in the neighbourhood with access to your house. Many cat owners will recognize the feeling of indignant surprise when they see a strange cat in the house, usually caught eating their cat's food. This can lead to feelings of insecurity in the home cat and problems with urine spraying, both with the home cat and the invading cat, as each tries to establish territory and assert its boundaries. One solution is to fix the flap on "exit-only", so that the cat can get out of the house but not back in. This is only a partial solution, however, as the cat could be left outside for long periods of time. Alternatively, there are more expensive magnetic or electronic flaps which will only open with an appropriate "key" device, which the cat has to wear attached to its collar. This is not totally satisfactory either, as cats will often lose their collars.

△ Radiator hammocks make a cosy retreat and are often favoured by ill or elderly cats, which feel the cold and dislike draughts.

◁ Some form of travelling basket is essential. Solid ones can make timid cats feel more secure.

▽ The open basket has the advantage of the cat being clearly visible, whilst reluctant cats are more easily removed from them.

▽ Secret hiding places like these are favoured by many cats. Timid cats will often use them to take refuge from the world for a few hours.

outdoor runs

Cats kept for breeding are not normally allowed the privilege of free roaming that most pets have. In these circumstances, a large outdoor run is a good idea, and will allow the cat to climb and play freely. The most important thing is to make sure that the run is secure. Cats are independent animals and do not appreciate being held captive against their will, and most will make a break for freedom if given the opportunity. There should always be a double-doored security passage between the enclosed run and freedom. If there is just the one door, sooner or later the agile, quick-thinking cat will escape to go off exploring. Even where two doors exist, it is not unknown for both of them to accidentally open at the same time and for the cat to escape. A breeding cat will need a dry, sheltered hut, rather like a small dog kennel, in its run. This needs to be kept well off the ground to stop the damp from coming up from underneath.

Feeding your cat

Cats are natural hunters. In the wild their diet would consist of small mammals, such as mice, shrews, voles, as well as birds and insects. This fare would be supplemented with plant seeds and leaves as desired. The cat is a solitary animal and, in a suitable habitat, will eat several small meals a day.

Ideally, your cat's diet should simulate this style of eating as closely as possible, although, practically speaking, it is unsuited for the majority of today's pet cats living in urban areas. Its long history as a hunter has developed the cat into an "obligate carnivore": it must eat animal protein in order to remain healthy. Cats need a total of 11 essential amino acids – the building blocks used to make protein – in their diet. These are found mainly in animal tissues, and one of them, taurine, is only found in meats. A lack of taurine in the diet can lead to blindness, heart disease and even death.

Cats have also developed the ability to use fats as a primary source of energy. In addition, fats are the main source of the essential fatty acids (EFAs) which are needed for their bodies to function properly. EFAs are more abundant in animal fats and fish oils than in plants, and there is one, arachidonic acid, which is hardly ever found in plants. It is important, therefore, that a cat's diet contains plenty of meat and fish.

It is best if you can feed your cat several small meals a day. The urine

▷ Commercial diets may be nutritionally balanced but a good home-made one is even better: you can then be sure what your cat is eating.

of a cat that is fed only once a day is more alkaline than that of one that gets three or four small meals. Minerals in the urine are more soluble in acid than in alkaline urine, so eating several small meals a day keeps the waste more acidic, thereby reducing the chance of stones forming in the bladder.

which type of diet?

A good home-prepared diet is preferable to a commercial one, as you are more able to give the cat the kind of diet it would get in the wild. The ideal diet would consist of something like 80 per cent raw chicken wings and 20 per cent liquidized green vegetables and overripe fruit. Offal can be used to replace some of the chicken, but liver should never make up more than ten per cent of the diet. Fish can also be substituted for part of the meat ration, but it should always be lightly cooked and deboned. Cooking is important

◁ After a meal a cat will usually settle down for a good grooming session and will emerge looking absolutely immaculate.

as it destroys the enzyme thiaminase, which can deactivate the cat's own Vitamin B1, thiamine. Eggs, too, can be added, but these should be cooked, as egg white can interfere with the absorption of biotin, another part of the Vitamin B complex.

With today's pressure on time and resources, it is likely that most cat owners will rely on commercially produced foods for their pet. It is perfectly acceptable to feed a fit cat on nothing but commercial diets. The foods are scientifically prepared to meet the cat's nutritional requirements in terms of carbohydrates, proteins, fats, vitamins and minerals. Most are complete diets, but some need extra supplements, so you should always check the label.

The animal foodstuff industry produces an increasingly wide range of convenience foods for all types of pet. Foods suitable for kittens, normal adult cats and the less energetic senior cat, are readily available in canned, semi-moist and dry kibble forms. Dry foods are cheaper than the canned ones and they weigh less, which means they are easy to transport. Both canned and dry foods will retain their nutritional goodness over a long period of time, and this makes bulk-buying a convenient option.

meat-based
canned food

all-in-one
complete food

kibble mixer

foil-wrapped,
semi-moist food

The quality of commercial diets may not be as high as we would like, however. The use of meatstuffs unfit for human consumption is banned in the United Kingdom, but not in many countries, including the United States. Animal protein can include reclaimed protein from parts of the animal that a human would not willingly eat, and many products add meat "flavouring" to improve the taste.

Remember that it is not unusual for cats to be fed in two or more homes: your cat may be getting extra food elsewhere. Consequently, an apparent loss of appetite is only significant if your cat appears very dull or is showing other signs of illness.

Clean fresh water should be available to your cat at all times. If your cat is one of those that prefers puddles to tap water, it may be because it doesn't like the taste of the chlorine and other additions to our water supply. If that is the case, you could try changing its water to bottled spring water or fresh rainwater. Ideally, stainless steel or ceramic bowls are better than plastic ones, as toxic compounds have been known to leach out of the plastic and into the water. In the wild, milk is not a part of the cat's diet. Although many cats like

milk, they do not actually need it. In fact many cats are sensitive to milk and, if your cat has a chronic bowel problem, milk is best avoided. Both food and water should be provided in bowls that are wider than the cat's whiskers. Cats find it easier to eat and drink from this type of container. For those owners who are out for most of the day, automatic feeding devices are available.

dietary supplements

Fit cats that are fed a good diet rarely need dietary supplements. *Brewer's yeast* is a good source of the Vitamin B complex, while 2.5 ml (½ tsp) *Cod Liver Oil* and *Evening Primrose Oil*, given twice-weekly, will help maintain levels of fat-soluble vitamins and the EFAs, especially arachidonic acid. Seaweed (kelp), available from health food stores in either powder or tablet form, is an excellent source of vitamins, minerals and amino acids. If you choose to prepare a home-made diet for your cat, try adding a handful of watercress and parsley, which are both high in vitamins and minerals,

▷ **Even well-fed cats will try to supplement their diet by hunting small rodents or birds. The fitter they are, the greater their chances of success.**

△ **Commercial diets come in many forms. All are designed to supply the cat's daily nutritional requirements when fed according to instructions.**

into the liquidized vegetable part of the diet. If you prefer to supplement a ready-made commercial diet, other than with *Brewer's yeast* and the oils mentioned above, check with your vet and let him or her recommend a suitable food supplement for your cat.

Exercise for cat health

A fit cat is a healthy cat. Exercise plays an important part in your pet's overall health and well-being. A cat needs the chance to run, pounce and climb freely. This stretches and strengthens its muscles, keeps its heart in good order, and maintains its lively and acute sensitivity.

Free-roaming cats have the chance to exercise, but many are lazy and do not make best use of the opportunity, often preferring to sun themselves in a warm spot rather than run about. It can also be difficult for an owner to get the balance right between freedom and safety, as many cats are killed or injured in road traffic accidents every year. It is possible to train some cats to walk on a collar and lead, but this is not ideal as a cat also needs some more dynamic form of movement.

In the wild, queens start to wean their young at about four weeks. They will bring in stunned, live prey for their kittens, who start to practise hunting skills at this age. Wild kittens will learn to kill mice from about five weeks. Most socializing skills are learnt at 7-12 weeks. If you have a kitten it will need lots of active play and attention. Kittens should not play for more than 15 minutes at any one time, but they need three short periods of playtime each day. Games that

◁ When your cat has caught its "prey", it should be allowed to play with it as a reward.

◁ Games that stimulate hunting activities provide a lot of amusement for both cat and owner.

teach hunting skills are obviously the best, and are also more likely to get a response from the kitten. A small ball can be used as "prey", but roll it past or away from the kitten, rather than towards it, so that it can chase it. An irregularly shaped ball, or a bias-weighted one that will roll irregularly, will bring more realism and interest to the game. Fishing-type toys are now made for cats, and these, too, are generally popular and bring variation to the game. Cat-nip toys can be bought or made for the kitten to play with. Like any child's toy, these should be checked for safety before they are given to the cat: look for small parts which could detach and get swallowed or cause injury.

At six months, the kitten's training in hunting and social skills will be complete. However, it is important to carry on playing with your cat throughout its life. Playing together helps to stabilize and reinforce the relationship between you and your cat. It will also bring a variety of experience into the cat's daily life, as well as being fun for both of you.

If your cat is a house cat, it is essential that it has enough scope for daily play and exercise indoors. Tower and tree-like objects are useful as they bring the play into three rather than two dimensions. They help to teach the cat co-ordination and strengthen muscles that may be under-exercised. Sophisticated modular climbing frames are available which can be changed around from time to time to provide a change of scene for the cat. They usually incorporate ledges, boxes to hide or rest in, and a carpeted or rope-covered scratching-post for sharpening claws. The physical

action of climbing will wear the claws and lessen the cat's need to scratch at furniture. Climbing frames are particularly useful for cats that are kept indoors all the time. If the cat does not have one of these, a scratching post at least 1 m high (1 yd) will be needed.

For breeding stock kept in outside runs, large branches and tree trunks should be provided to give the cat a chance of vertical movements as well as ground-level exercise. A wide variety of hanging and moveable toys should be available, which should be changed regularly to prevent boredom.

Try to make your home safe for your cat. Upper windows and high balconies should be made cat-proof. Cats have incredible balance, but they do fall from such places. This is not usually from a lack of balance but, more likely, from chasing insects or from sleeping on a narrow ledge and rolling over the wrong way. Cats have remarkable righting reflexes and always seem to land on their feet, but if they fall from a great height, the impact can be enough to break legs.

△ Obesity restricts the physical activity of a cat and will seriously reduce its desire to play.

House-training kittens

For the first few months of their lives, kittens will be groomed and cleaned by their mother. Somewhere between three and six weeks, a kitten will begin to look for materials similar to those used by its mother to urinate and defecate on; this is usually something open and well-drained. Not all cats cover their eliminations, but if they are going to, they will start at about seven weeks, when their sense of smell becomes fully developed.

◁ Many types of cat litter are available. If a cat refuses to use its tray, try changing the litter type in the first instance.

litter tray

When homing a kitten, try to use the same or a very similar material in a litter tray as its mother was using. The kitten should then take to it readily. The litter tray must be large enough for a full-grown cat to be able to squat in it easily. It is best placed on a large sheet of paper in case of accidents. If the kitten is not house-trained when you get it, remember that it will eliminate urine and faeces several times a day, usually 15–20 minutes after eating. Watch the kitten after feeding time and when it begins to squat or looks like it needs to go to the toilet, pick it up and put it on the tray. Keep an old towel handy and put it under its rump as you pick it up to protect yourself from any accidents. Always praise your kitten when it uses its tray properly, and give it a treat to reinforce the use of the tray.

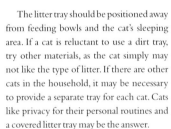

▷ Wearing rubber gloves when cleaning the litter tray will prevent owners, particularly pregnant women, from catching diseases such as toxoplasmosis from the faeces.

The litter tray should be positioned away from feeding bowls and the cat's sleeping area. If a cat is reluctant to use a dirt tray, try other materials, as the cat simply may not like the type of litter. If there are other cats in the household, it may be necessary to provide a separate tray for each cat. Cats like privacy for their personal routines and a covered litter tray may be the answer.

If you have rehomed a stray or rescued adult cat, it, too, may need house-training. Wait with the cat after meals and place it on the litter tray when it begins to squat. If you are having trouble getting a rehomed adult cat to use a tray, try different litter materials. The cat should be praised and given a treat after correct use of the tray.

keeping clean

Litter trays should be cleaned regularly. Cats prefer to be clean and they dislike dirty trays. Some will not use a tray that other cats have used, while others will refuse their own tray if they have soiled it once. Always wear rubber gloves when cleaning the cat's tray, especially if you are pregnant, because of the risk of disease transferred from prey.

As cats use urine and faeces to mark their territory, traces of either found in the house could mean that your cat feels threatened by a newcomer in its area. It could also be the first sign of a urinary tract infection or incontinence. If the soiling is persistent, you should see the vet.

▷ Your cat may refuse to use its litter tray if an intruding cat has entered the house and soiled it.

Daily grooming for your cat

Depending on its breed, cats may be long- or short-haired. Whatever the length of its fur, however, a cat's coat should always be dirt-free and shining. Almost without exception, cats are clean animals and are particular about their grooming rituals.

◁ Cats groom themselves several times a day to keep their coats in good order, using their teeth, tongue and paws as tools.

natural cleaning

Cats spend considerable amounts of time washing and grooming themselves. A cat will clean its coat using its tongue as a comb, and will clean around its eyes and ears – the parts it cannot reach with its tongue – using its front feet. If you look at a cat's tongue you will see that the top surface is covered in tiny, backward-projecting, spikes. These spikes act like a comb. The cat's tongue untangles any matted hairs and removes loose ones. Since these spikes point backwards, any hairs caught up in them can only move backwards down the throat, where they are swallowed. They pass into the stomach and are finally eliminated from the body with the faeces. If excessive quantities of loose hairs gather in the stomach, they build up into furballs which the cat will regurgitate.

With the long-haired breeds, the cat's tongue may be incapable of coping with the knots that form in the fur. These knots grow slowly and can develop into large felted mats. Once the hair has begun to mat, it can be very difficult to untangle.

If a cat resents the pulling needed to remove the knots, it may be best to take the cat to a vet, who will give it an anaesthetic before removing the knots. Sometimes it is necessary to carefully cut the knots away. Long-haired cats may need two or more grooming sessions a day, especially in bad weather, to prevent the build-up of mats.

daily routine

The best time to start grooming your cat is before it needs it, to avoid more drastic measures. Kittens are used to being groomed by their mothers, so if you get your cat as a kitten, start grooming sessions straight away. Some cats, especially rescued stray or semi-wild cats, do not have enough trust in humans to allow stroking or grooming, so you may need to get the cat used to being handled before you can groom it.

In cats which are tolerant enough to allow it, a daily grooming session has many benefits. It helps to remove the loose hairs

for the cat, preventing any future furball problems. If the cat is long-haired, any knots in its coat can be gently untangled so that mats do not form. Grooming also helps to strengthen the bond between you and your cat. Establish a routine early on.

A fine-toothed metal comb is the best tool to use for both short- and long-haired cats. Although brushing the fur may make it look good on the surface, the bristles tend not to get down to skin level, leaving the layer of hair next to the skin untouched. This encourages knots to start forming in long-haired cats. Untangle the coat first with a comb, then finish with a brush to bring up the shine, if the cat will allow it.

First remove any knots and/or vegetable matter, such as leaves and twigs, that may be lodged in the skin or fur. Then start at the head and check the eyes, ears and nose for abnormal smells. If there are any discharges, these should be cleaned away using moist cotton wool balls (cotton balls).

Get your cat used to having its mouth opened and looked into. This will help if you ever need to give it any medication. If there is a nasty smell from its mouth, check for bones or other foreign objects that might be stuck between the teeth or in the soft tissues of its mouth. Look for ulcers which may be starting to form on its lips. Check also for the presence of tartar. If tartar is allowed to build up, it will irritate

◁ Many types of brush and comb are available. The breeder where you buy your cat will help you select the right ones to use.

Time spent grooming your cat is never wasted. Establish a grooming routine as early as possible in your pet's life. If you start when it is young, and not much interference is needed, the cat is more likely to tolerate your efforts. The fur, particularly of long-haired cats, can mat so much that shaving is the only way to deal with it.

◁ **1** When grooming the cat's face, clean away all discharges from the eyes, nose and mouth, using damp cotton wool (cotton balls). Gently tease or cut away any mats that are present in the fur.

▽ **2** Generally, metal combs are more effective than brushes for long-haired cats because they will penetrate the fur down to skin level. Always check the fur for twigs, leaves and knots when combing.

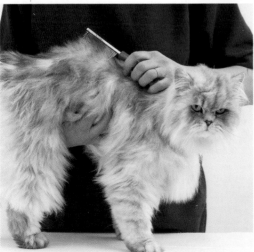

◁ **3** If the coat is badly matted, it may be easier to work forward from the tail, making sure you get right to the root of any knot.

△ **4** Don't forget to check the mouth for nasty smells. The teeth should be checked, too, for excess tartar, and the gums for any signs of ulceration.

the gums and lead to dental problems. Toothbrushes and flavoured non-foaming toothpastes are now available for cats.

Next, comb along the lie of the cat's coat, towards the tail. As well as the back, comb down the sides and the underside. If it will let you, it is best to roll the cat over to expose its tummy area. Knots often start in the armpit and groin areas and these can be overlooked if the cat remains upright. While combing, check for signs of injuries, such as cuts, bites, and painful joints. Look for any greasy areas, spots and lumps that could indicate skin disease. If there is any oil on the coat, you should take the cat to the vet as soon as possible: oil will quickly penetrate a cat's highly absorbent skin, causing liver damage, which can be serious.

Worming your cat

Cats, like all other mammals, are subject to intestinal worms. It is probably true that the natural state of any mammal is to have a few worms. When the cat is run down, poorly fed or suffering from disease, however, then worms can become a problem.

Cats may carry both tapeworms and roundworms. Tapeworms exist in two forms: as a cyst or as a flat tapeworm. Prey animals, such as mice and birds, and cat fleas all carry tapeworm cysts. When a cat ingests a cyst, it develops into a flat tapeworm which buds off into segments when it is mature. The segments then appear, either in the faeces, or else sticking to the hairs in the anal region of the cat. These tapeworms are not normally of any risk to humans but they can be very debilitating to cats.

There are several varieties of round-worm that can affect cats, and more often than not, kittens are born with them. The commonest roundworm seen in cats can also infect humans. It has a complicated five-stage development cycle, during which it passes round the body in the bloodstream. Should a human accidentally eat an infected egg, the egg does not develop properly but will go astray in the bloodstream, usually ending up as a cyst in a muscle. On very rare occasions, it can travel to the retina at the back of the eye, and cause blindness. As cats are usually careful to bury their faeces, it is very unusual for a human to catch a roundworm from a cat, and more unusual still for it to cause any harm. However, because of the risk to human health, all kittens should be routinely wormed at least three times when they are young, and grown cats should still be treated regularly.

Although complementary medicines can help to eliminate worms and will offer some protection against re-infestation, they are not as efficient or reliable at killing worms as pharmaceutical medicines. The wormers available from vets are designed to protect against round- and tapeworms, and are safer and more effective than the

△ **Some cats will happily eat up their worming powder if it has been sprinkled over their food.**

wormers sold in pet shops. The wormers come in tablet, liquid and granular form. Theoretically, they can be given neat or mixed with food, but in reality they can be difficult to give to cats, who will often just refuse to eat "worm-treated" food. As an alternative, an injectable tapeworm medicine is now available from vets.

It is usually sufficient to treat cats for roundworms every six months, unless there are young children in the house, in which case it is best to treat them every three months. Most cats only need treating for tapeworms when worm-segments are seen. However, if your cat regularly catches birds and small mammals, it will need routine worming every three months.

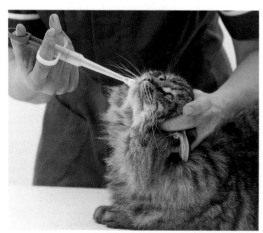

△ **Worming treatments can be given orally, by professional staff at the vet's surgery, to cats who are reluctant to take tablets of any shape or form.**

COMPLEMENTARY TREATMENT

Probably the best use of complementary treatment is for the cat who is continually troubled by worms. In such cases, holistic treatment may help to both reduce the cat's susceptibility to picking up worms and also help to repel them. *Garlic* in its herbal form can be used; homeopathic *Cina 30C* helps to eliminate roundworms from irritable animals, and *Abrotanum 6C* helps if there is marked weight loss in an otherwise fit animal. These remedies can be given twice daily for up to one week. For tapeworms, *Filix mas. 3X* is useful when the cat is constipated and *Granatum 3X* if there is weight loss. Massage with essential oils of *Marjoram* or *Thyme* is said to be helpful, but aromatherapy is difficult in cats as they tend not to like strong smells on their fur. The tissue salt *Natrum phos.* may also be useful for worm infestations.

Kitten vaccinations

In recent years, the vaccination of cats has become more popular. The three most common vaccines give protection against feline infectious enteritis (FIE), feline influenza (cat flu) and feline leukaemia (FeLV). An initial course of two injections, the first at nine weeks and the second at 12 weeks are usually given, and yearly boosters are recommended thereafter.

FIE causes vomiting and diarrhoea, and the cat develops a very high temperature. Before the vaccine was introduced, it killed a great many cats by dehydration due to the bowel symptoms. Cat flu is caused by two viruses: the feline rhinotracheitis virus (FVR) and the feline calici virus (FCV). FVR is the more severe of the two, causing coughing, sneezing, and nasal and eye discharges. FCV has milder discharges but more gum inflammation and mouth ulcers. Neither FCV nor FVR is usually fatal but the infection can linger on in the form of snuffles, and some cats become symptomless carriers of the disease. When stressed, these cats develop mild symptoms and spread the virus. This explains outbreaks of cat flu in catteries when all the cats inside have been vaccinated against the disease.

◁ **Kittens should be vaccinated at about 12 weeks of age. In the United Kingdom, the injection is given into the scruff; in the United States sites on the legs are preferred.**

FeLV suppresses the activity of the cat's immune system, allowing a wide range of symptoms to develop. It often results in the death of the cat after several months of illness. The virus is spread mainly in the cat's saliva. It is a disease of cats that fight a lot, and of cats in large colonies, who share the same food and water bowls. It should not be a threat in a well-run boarding cattery, where the feeding and grooming utensils are properly cleaned, and the cats do not mix with each other.

A vaccine exists against the chlamydial organism, which can cause not only mild eye and nasal symptoms but, more importantly, infertility and abortion. This vaccine is used mainly in breeding colonies to protect against infertility.

△ **All kittens should be vaccinated in the usual way until an effective alternative is found.**

COMPLEMENTARY TREATMENT

According to homeopathic theory, medicines made from the diseased tissues or discharges of infected animals (nosodes) can be used to give immunity. However, these medicines have not been tested because the homeopathic community objects to experiments which could be potentially lethal for the unprotected test animals. After a conventional vaccination, the level of circulating antibodies (CAB) in the bloodstream rises, which indicates that the vaccine has worked. There is no rise in the CAB level after nosode administration, however, and this is taken as proof that nosodes are ineffective. An English veterinary homeopath, George MacLeod, claimed that there was a change in the Opsonic Index (OI) after nosode treatment. The OI measures the ability of the white blood cells to destroy bacteria, but changes in the OI are difficult to measure. It is an expensive way to record the results of nosode treatment, and because of this its commercial potential is limited. There is a small body of work that supports the use of nosodes in a preventative role, but you are advised to talk the matter over with a homeopathically-trained vet if you are considering nosode administration as an alternative to conventional vaccines. It is also unlikely that homeopathic "immunization" would be regarded as valid by most cattery owners, who have to consider the safety of the other animals in their care.

Neutering and contraception

Reproduction is an essential part of life, and the sex hormones have a major effect on the function of both body and mind. Removal of the reproductive organs and the body's ability to produce sex hormones can have profound effects on humans. It may be reasonable to assume that cats are affected in similar ways.

However, in today's world, some form of contraception is essential in cats. They reproduce so quickly and easily that we would soon be overrun by unwanted kittens, and this would only increase the number of unwanted cats that have to be given euthanasia or else become strays. It is impractical to use physical separation as a method of feline contraception if a cat is to be given the freedom to roam outdoors alone. This leaves sterilization as the only humane option.

Many animal charities like to neuter cats as early as possible (at three to four months) to make sure the cats do not reproduce after they have been rehomed. However, a cat's body development is controlled by its sex hormones, and the females will look more feminine and the males more masculine

◁ An un-neutered tom cat will brazenly spray his urine to assert his presence as part of the mating ritual. Most owners find this habit unpleasant, and it can become difficult to deal with in areas inhabited by the family.

if neutering can be left until five and six months respectively. With today's modern anaesthetics there is no difference in surgical risk to the cat at either age.

female sterilization

The cat's reproductive cycle is designed for efficiency. A mature queen's follicles ripen but do not burst and release the egg until after she has been physically mated by a tom. When she needs to be mated, she will

call for a tom until mating occurs. Isolating a queen from tom cats is not a practical option, and sterilization is strongly recommended by most vets. This can be done using chemical methods, where tablets can prevent the follicles forming, or through surgery (spaying).

For the average house cat, spaying before six months, or before she starts calling, is the best option. If the cat has already started calling, hormone tablets can be given to a

---

CASTRATION

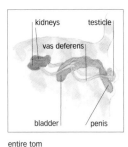

kidneys   testicle
vas deferens
bladder   penis

entire tom

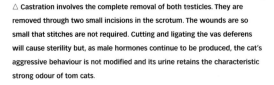

castrated tom

△ Castration involves the complete removal of both testicles. They are removed through two small incisions in the scrotum. The wounds are so small that stitches are not required. Cutting and ligating the vas deferens will cause sterility but, as male hormones continue to be produced, the cat's aggressive behaviour is not modified and its urine retains the characteristic strong odour of tom cats.

SPAYING

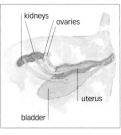

kidneys   ovaries
uterus
bladder

entire queen

spayed queen

△ A total ovario-hysterectomy is the preferred way to spay female cats. This not only causes sterility but it also eliminates the queen's desire to mate. A simple hysterectomy or the ligation of the fallopian tubes would also cause sterility, but it would not stop her from producing the female hormones, and she would continue to call in order to attract entire tom cats until mating occurred.

▷ Entire toms are staunch defenders of their land, and will react aggressively towards any visitor seen as a threat to their dominance.

sage

△ Massage with diluted essential oil of sage can help after operations on the female organs.

mature queen to stop the calling and avoid putting her undue stress (prolonged calling may cause exhaustion and depression). If the queen has not been spayed before she starts to call, it is best left until ten days after she stops calling, because she will take better to the anaesthetic and surgery is safer when her hormone activity is low.

male sterilization

Toms not wanted for breeding purposes should be neutered (castrated) before they are six months old. Apart from creating unwanted kittens, un-neutered toms will fight other toms as part of the mating ritual. This makes them subject to nasty bites and increases their chances of contacting FeLV. The waste products of the male hormones give a unique odour to an adult tom's urine, and most people find this objectionable in and around the home. A neutered tom will also be more affectionate by nature.

△ Queens are very prolific. They are capable of having four or five litters, each of four or five kittens, every year. A queen with one kitten is quite a rarity.

△ Un-neutered toms are formidable fighting machines, and are often battle-scarred.

Reproduction in a healthy cat

Cats do not usually become sexually mature before they are six months old, although some queens may start calling a month or so earlier. A queen born in the autumn may not mature until the following spring and may not begin to call until she is seven or eight months old. Once a queen starts to call, she calls for between five and ten days, every three weeks, until she is mated.

should I breed from my cat?

Today, the majority of cats are neutered, and the number of unwanted street cats is declining, whilst the number of pedigree cats is rising. If you are considering letting your queen have kittens, you should think it through before letting her be mated.

Some owners plan to have their pet queen spayed but wish to let her have at least one litter of kittens beforehand. Remember that mating involves fighting, not all queens take to motherhood, and a significant percentage suffer emotional problems when their kittens are rehomed. It doesn't seem to make much difference if the queen has had kittens or not: she may or may not react badly to being spayed.

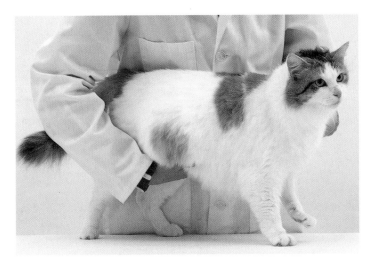

If you own a pedigree queen, you may want to breed from her specifically to sell the kittens. However, commercially breeding cats requires commitment on the part of the owner. To begin with, you will need to find a suitable stud-tom, and pay a sizeable fee for his services. The queen will need extra feeding in the last third of her pregnancy, and her kittens will need feeding until they are rehomed at 12 weeks. A suitable kittening box must be provided for the birth and a suitable exercise area for the kittens for the next 12 weeks. The cost of worming the mother before and after kittening, and the kittens themselves, three times after birth, must be allowed for. Not all pregnancies go according to plan: if a Caesarean section is required, there will be extra vet's fees; if there are stillbirths, there will be no kittens to sell. Pedigree kittens which sell for high prices are usually parented by a queen or stud-tom that has a successful show record, and have been bred by professional cat-breeders.

If you decide you would like your queen to have kittens, talk it over with the vet and, if she is a pedigree, with the breeder from whom you bought her. The vet can advise

△ **Your vet can often feel the foetuses in the uterus during the fourth week of pregnancy. Blood tests are not yet available for cats.**

you on the health risks of breeding, whilst the breeder can help with the selection of a suitable stud-tom and some of the more practical preparations that need to be made. Most breeders demand that visiting queens are blood-tested for FeLV before they will allow their tom to mate them.

pregnancy and birth

Queens carry their kittens for approximately 63 days, although the kittens can come up to two days early or three days late. Let your vet know when your queen has been mated so that he can make a note of her dates. He may need to make himself available at short notice later on. He can also make a manual pregnancy diagnosis, which is 90 per cent accurate, between the 22nd and 28th days. More accurate pregnancy diagnosis can be done using an ultra-sonic scanner from about the sixth week.

The use of a *Raspberry Leaf* infusion, given daily during the pregnancy, will help to tone the uterus and strengthen the

△ **The Bach Flower mustard can help to lift any feelings of melancholy that may be seen in the queen after the rehoming of her kittens.**

▷ The queen should break the membranes and clean the kittens immediately after birth; if she does not, you will have to help her.

contractions when the queen is at full term. Alternatively, homeopathic *Caulophyllum 30C* can be given weekly for the last three weeks of pregnancy and every 15 minutes for up to four doses when labour begins.

preparing a kittening box

The queen will need a safe, private place in which to have her kittens: a kittening box is ideal, and this can be prepared in advance. The box can be made from a large, lidded cardboard box with a hole for access cut in to the side. You need to be able to lift the

raspberry leaf

△ Raspberry leaf infusions are the traditional herbal tonic for the female tract, and will greatly benefit a queen during her pregnancy.

top of the box off easily, in case there is a need for assistance at the birth. The queen should be introduced to the box three weeks before her due date so that she is familiar with it, and is comfortable in her artificial cave. Cats are very private creatures and without this precaution she may look for shelter under (or worse still, in) your bed, or under a wardrobe. She may even go away to have her kittens on her own if she can't find a suitable place in the house. When the birth is imminent, the box can be lined with several layers of clean newspaper which can be removed and burnt, layer by layer, as they become messy.

the delivery

Queens tend to give birth at night, and you may wake up in the morning to a litter of new-born kittens. Alternatively, the cat may seek your company or attract it by her behaviour or by making a noise. Even if she seems to want solitude, try to stay within sight so that you can help her if necessary.

The first stage of labour is not dramatic. The queen may appear restless or uncomfortable and may breathe a little more deeply than usual. When she is ready to

deliver her kittens, she will sit up and begin to push hard. If she pushes hard for more than half an hour and no kitten is born, or if there is a big gush of fluid, or part of a kitten appears and the kitten is not born within half an hour, assistance may be needed. If no more happens during that time, you should ring the vet.

If the queen ignores the kittens, you will need to break the membranes to allow the kittens to breathe, clearing their mouths if they are full of mucus. Hold each kitten in the palm of your hands and swing it head down, with the neck supported by your fingers: this will remove any stubborn mucus. Break the cord 2.5 cm (1 in) from the umbilicus after two minutes, and dry the kitten by rubbing vigorously with a clean, rough towel. This helps to stimulate its breathing.

If the queen has her kittens in quick succession, your help is almost certainly going to be needed as she will not have time to attend to each one individually. Make sure the kittens are dried quickly and do not get chilled. After kittening, the queen can be given three doses of homeopathic *Arnica* every two hours.

Holistic Therapies

When internal energies are able to circulate smoothly
and freely, and the energy of the mind is not scattered,
but it is focused and concentrated, illness and disease
can be avoided.

The Yellow Emperor's Classic of Medicine, 250BC

an alternative view

The basic philosophy underlying holistic medicine is a concern for the living totality of the patient. Its aim is to treat the patient as a whole and not the disease in isolation.

the whole cat

Holistic treatment is not aimed at the cause of infection or the suppression of symptoms, but at all aspects of the cat's life, including its mental and emotional state, co-existing physical complaints, lifestyle stresses and nutritional status. Western medicine looks for the name of the disease (the diagnosis) and for the one correct treatment to cure the symptoms. Holistic medicine looks at a wider concept of dis-ease. It recognizes that a number of treatments may be needed, from simple lifestyle changes to surgery and conventional medicines. It also accepts that therapies that cannot be explained by science can affect the whole organism, and are often needed to achieve a cure.

where to get treatment

In human medicine, there are now many holistic clinics where patients are treated by teams of therapists under the supervision of a doctor. In the veterinary field, things are not so sophisticated. There is a growing number of veterinary practices worldwide offering holistic therapies, but the range of services available is still very limited.

There are also legal restraints in holistic practice for animals. The law recognizes that humans understand the risks involved in seeking non-medically qualified treatment. Because an animal is incapable of assessing risk, the treatment of disease in animals is restricted to veterinary surgeons only. Vets are allowed to work alongside qualified, animal-trained physiotherapists, osteopaths and chiropractors, but the more esoteric therapies can only be carried out by the cat's owner, or by vets who are suitably qualified – and of these there are very few.

If you wish to use holistic therapies on your cat, discuss the matter first with your vet. This way, any essential conventional care can be given before a holistic treatment plan is worked out between you.

therapies for cats

Of the therapies suitable for cats and other animals, homeopathy and acupuncture are the most common. These are complete systems of medicine, and each has its own philosophy. Both see disease as an imbalance of energy. Homeopathy recognizes a "Vital Force" in the body which attempts to keep the body in good health. Disease is seen as a disturbance of that force, and the symptoms as the body's attempt to regain equilibrium. The symptoms are then used to find the one, curative medicine. Homeopathy also

believes that lifestyle circumstances may predispose us to disease, and that these must be eliminated if a true cure is to result.

Acupuncture is a branch of Traditional Chinese Medicine (TCM). This system sees energy as flowing round the body along channels known as meridians. Disease occurs when this energy flow is disturbed. Stimulation of specific points on the body's meridians restores balance to the system and health to the body.

Ayurvedic medicine is an Indian holistic system with its own philosophy of disease. It recognizes a flow of energy, which it calls prana through channels known as nadis. The major nadis have energy vortices or chakras. Treatment is based on herbal medicine and diet. Ayurvedic medicine is far less common in the Western world than acupuncture and homeopathy.

Complementary therapies which work at the energy level include the Bach Flower remedies and crystal therapy. The Bach Flowers are chosen on the basis of the cat's emotional state. Crystal therapy attempts to use the energy given off by crystals to restore balance to the energy field of the body.

Other widely practised holistic therapies include herbalism, aromatherapy, massage, physiotherapy, osteopathy and chiropractic. Orthodox science, in general, is more ready to accept therapies with a physical basis.

▷ An inquisitive cat will not be able to resist a sniff at an essential oil bottle. If the cat recoils in horror, do not force it to go back for more.

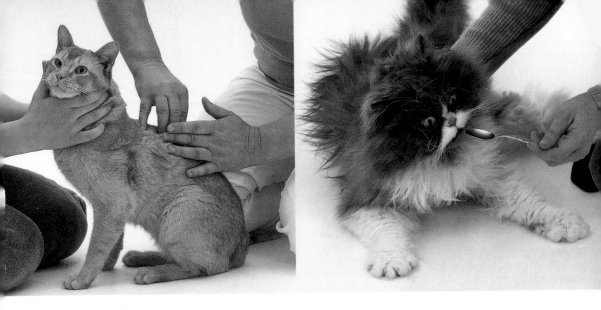

△ Osteopathic and chiropractic manipulation help back and limb problems. Homeopathic remedies can usually be given easily to cats, and can be helpful for injuries and chronic diseases. Acupuncture is used mainly for musculoskeletal problems and for skin and respiratory complaints. The Bach Flower remedies are also easily given, and can be used at home to support all conventional treatments. Aromatherapy should be used with care because of the cat's highly developed sense of smell.

Physical therapies: massage

Massage is probably one of the oldest and simplest therapy techniques of all. When a child hurts itself, a parent's instinctive reaction is to "rub it better". In the womb, the skin develops from the same cell layer as the nervous system and the two are closely connected. This may explain why massage calms the mind as well as the body, and gives a sense of complete well-being.

positive effects

Cats, in general, like to be rubbed, stroked and massaged, and will often seek out their owners for this kind of attention. A cat will convey its pleasure by purring and kneading its claws. When you massage your cat, you are establishing a non-verbal communication that conveys an attitude of loving care. This strengthens the bond that exists between you and your pet, and increases trust. The resulting feeling of harmony is not only physically soothing, but it will promote mental and emotional strength which will help to guard the cat against disease.

Massage has many beneficial effects on the physical body. By stimulating the circulation, it relaxes the muscles, helps to balance joint action and muscle function, and speeds the dispersal of scar tissue. The improved circulation also speeds up the rate at which the lymphatic system detoxifies the body. Finally, massage will increase the production of the body's natural painkillers (endorphins), which optimize a feeling of well-being. The act of giving a massage is also extremely therapeutic, and studies have shown that it can help to reduce the stress and blood pressure levels of the masseur, in addition to the effect on the patient.

a basic routine

Begin with a few long, gentle strokes of even pressure along the body and limbs, in the same direction as the hair growth. The strokes should be slow and rhythmic and will help to relax the cat. They also allow you to locate any tender spots. Lubricants are not normally necessary. If lubrication is needed, use baby powder and not one of the vegetable-based oils used in human massage. Oils make the fingers slide too quickly over the skin for the massage to be effective. They are also very messy on fur, and will penetrate easily into the skin, which in a cat is highly absorbent.

Cats are private, sensitive creatures who do not like attention forced on them, and they may be suspicious of your first attempts at massage. If this is the case, do not persist, but stop as soon as the animal indicates that it has had enough.

If the cat allows it, increase the pressure of each stroke and change the direction towards the heart to stimulate venous and lymphatic drainage. Ideally, the massage should start at the feet and move upwards towards the head. Cats which have particularly sensitive feet may resent having them handled. In this case, start the massage at the head and work down the body, stroking upwards all the time.

If you can start at the feet, massage slowly and gently, putting your fingers in the spaces between the toes. Then use your fingers to massage the legs, upwards towards the body, beginning just above the paw. If the cat will allow it, get it to roll over and massage its tummy, using a circular motion. If not, turn your attention to its back and chest, using your palms, if possible, or your fingers. Starting at the tail-end and using circular movements, massage along one side, working forwards to the head, before moving to the other side.

Never massage directly on to the cat's spine. Instead, use your fingertips on the muscle groups on each side, where muscle trigger points may exist. These points cause

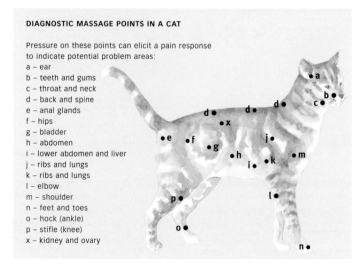

DIAGNOSTIC MASSAGE POINTS IN A CAT

Pressure on these points can elicit a pain response to indicate potential problem areas:

a – ear
b – teeth and gums
c – throat and neck
d – back and spine
e – anal glands
f – hips
g – bladder
h – abdomen
i – lower abdomen and liver
j – ribs and lungs
k – ribs and lungs
l – elbow
m – shoulder
n – feet and toes
o – hock (ankle)
p – stifle (knee)
x – kidney and ovary

Simple massage

Cats are tactile creatures and usually enjoy receiving the attention that goes with a massage. The experience may bring therapeutic benefits to you as well, and a regular massage will help to strengthen the bond between you and your cat. Add the massage to the end of the daily grooming session.

△ **1** Try to start with the cat's feet and legs. This will stimulate the flow of blood and lymph back to the heart. Be smooth and gentle, and work carefully into the spaces between the cat's toes.

△ **2** Work up the hind legs to the hip and up the front legs to the shoulder. Keep the movements firm but smooth, using your fingers or palm.

△ **3** The back muscles often contain trigger points that cause the surrounding muscles to go into a reflex spasm. Any tight band of muscle should only be massaged lightly to help relax it; vigorous massage will increase the contraction and cause pain.

△ **4** End the session with gentle strokes over the whole head area. This part of the session is usually greatly enjoyed by the cat.

the surrounding muscles to contract or go into spasm as a protective reflex. The bands of tight muscle can be felt with skilled fingers. They should be lightly massaged so as to reduce the reactivity of the point and relax the tight muscles. Firm finger pressure

on the point itself can deactivate it, but any vigorous massage can increase pain.

Finally, move to the head and neck. You can massage all parts of the head, including around the eyes, nose, mouth and ears. Touch gently with your fingertips, paying

particular attention to any region that seems to give the cat extra comfort. The neck should be treated as an extension of the back, and massaged on each side of the spine. End the sequence with a few light strokes from head to tail.

Physical therapies: physiotherapy

This therapy supplements the medical and surgical treatment of conditions that have a major impact on the musculoskeletal, or locomotor, system and the circulation. It plays an important part in mainstream medicine and is also a vital component of holistic medicine.

what is physiotherapy?

Physiotherapy aims to regain the strength and full range of movement of an injured area by manual manipulation or by a series of controlled exercises. It can help to control pain, speed up healing, and preserve the function of injured tissue. It can be used alongside surgery, pharmaceutical medicines and all complementary therapies. Veterinary physiotherapy is routinely performed on professional sports animals, such as racehorses and greyhounds, and is slowly becoming more widely used in general veterinary practice.

Simple massage, the use of ice-packs and gentle warmth may be tried by owners as self-help treatments at home. However, the more specialist physiotherapy techniques can inflict further injury if misapplied, and these should only ever be used by a qualified physiotherapist.

how it works

Treatment is achieved by manual manipulation or by a series of controlled exercises. The treatment is supported by the use of cold and heat, electrical stimulation and laser therapy. It is particularly useful with cats who have been involved in severe road

◁ Stroke your hands down the cat's back to relax your pet with a massage. Relaxation of the damaged area will encourage the reduction of swelling, pain and tension.

traffic accidents, although in general cats are not used to being exercised and will not tolerate much in the way of manipulation.

The therapeutic use of cold is applied as quickly as possible after an injury, in the form of a cold compress to reduce the seepage of blood and other fluids into the surrounding tissue. This will also decrease muscle spasms and reduces nerve pain. A plastic beaker filled with water and frozen, or a packet of frozen vegetables, could both be used at home as a cold compress on large

areas and surgical wounds. The compress should be used 2–4 times a day, for up to 20 minutes at a time.

Therapeutic warmth is used 72 hours after an injury to increase blood circulation in the damaged tissue. Warmth also helps to remove waste products and increases nourishment of the area, speeding up the healing, and relieving tension and pain.

Electrical stimulation has a variety of benefits. Special equipment can be used to help with pain relief and to stimulate muscle

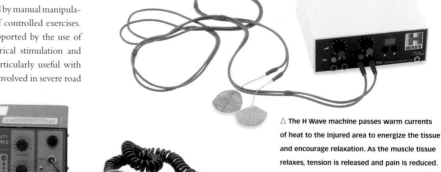

△ The H Wave machine passes warm currents of heat to the injured area to energize the tissue and encourage relaxation. As the muscle tissue relaxes, tension is released and pain is reduced.

◁ Lasers uses light energy to stimulate tissue circulation in muscle. Increasing the circulation relaxes muscle tension to speed healing.

◁ Pressure point work, using the thumbs, can be done at home. Work on musculature to relieve pain and tension by enhancing the blood circulation.

contractions. The latter can help to counteract muscle wastage, reduce spasm pains and increase muscle strength. It can also increase blood flow in damaged tissue and where there are certain forms of circulatory disease. This also aids healing.

Ultrasound is used to provide heat therapy by using the energy of ultrasonic vibrations to warm the tissues beneath the skin, which helps to increase the amount by which scar and other fibrous tissue can stretch. This allows the remodelling of scar tissue and helps to reduce the amount of scar tissue that does form. It can also help to deactivate painful muscular trigger points when used by trained operatives. Ultrasound treatment must never be used after exercise: it can have the opposite effect of increasing pain by overheating the tissue, causing further damage to the area.

As part of their treatment, a physiotherapist will normally suggest suitable exercises to help the cat's recovery. However, it can be difficult to use controlled exercise with cats, although stretching is useful when the cat is recuperating from injuries. Physiotherapists will use their knowledge of the cat's anatomy to perform manually assisted stretches once the cat's muscles have been warmed up by gentle exercise.

availability

Qualified physiotherapists are registered and legally recognized. Once a medical diagnosis has been made by your vet, the physiotherapist will treat the cat under the vet's direction. In order to practise on animals, some physiotherapists undertake additional veterinary training. If you or your vet think that physiotherapy would be beneficial for your cat, try to enlist the help of a qualified veterinary physiotherapist: they will be more familiar with the cat's anatomy and will be more able to handle the animal. The independent nature of cats means that many will resent treatment.

△ Pull your cat's hind leg backwards to gently stretch the injured limb. This maintains the range of movement and will help to prevent stiffness.

△ Hold a packet of frozen vegetables against the injured area as a cold compress to reduce damage in the area immediately surrounding the injury.

Physical therapies: osteopathy

This is a form of treatment based on the manipulation of the body's bony skeleton. Its basic premise is that imbalance and disharmony will result from the changes that occur in all parts of the body when one part of its structure is altered. Osteopathy is not a complete system of medicine.

what is osteopathy?

Osteopathy was developed in the late 19th century by an American, Dr Andrew Taylor Still. He saw the skeleton as having a dual purpose. The commonly recognized function was that it provided the physical framework for the body. By the action of the muscles that were attached to it, it allowed the mechanical movement of the body. Its other, equally important, function was to protect the body's vital organs. Dr Still theorized that if the skeleton were out of alignment, the body it supported and protected would not be able to maintain a state of good health. The basis of osteopathy is that structure governs function.

▷ Cats will benefit greatly from osteopathy following falls or road accidents.

Osteopathy is used alongside orthodox Western medicine. Osteopaths are trained to treat each patient as a complete structure, paying close attention to the relationship between the musculoskeletal system and the function of the body. They look at a patient's history to decide if osteopathy is a suitable treatment. A thorough physical examination enables them to observe the ease and range of movement in the limbs and spine. By feeling the muscles and bones, the osteopath can locate painful areas and identify any misalignments of the skeleton. The osteopath is then able to make a diagnosis and develop a treatment plan.

how it works

Osteopathy on cats uses soft-tissue massage techniques and joint manipulations to make adjustments to the damaged neuro-musculoskeletal structure. The techniques used on cats and humans are very similar. Manipulation techniques make corrections which repair the damage and allow healing to occur. After the initial treatment, the osteopath will monitor improvements by sight and by feeling the changes that occur in the diseased area and in the body.

Osteopathic massage increases blood flow, which speeds up the elimination of toxic waste products that build up in the damaged areas. It increases the oxygenation of the tissues to relieve pain and stiffness.

The most common joint-manipulation technique used in osteopathy is the high-velocity thrust. Contrary to popular belief, although this causes popping noises, it does not realign bones and joints. It does, however, slightly separate the joint surfaces momentarily. This separation stretches the joint capsule and gives it greater freedom of movement. As the joint capsule is stretched, tiny bubbles of carbon dioxide come out of solution from the joint fluid and these are responsible for the popping sound.

The other techniques used are passive movement and articulation. These gently and painlessly stretch the soft tissues to result in greater joint and limb mobility. Passive movement involves the osteopath moving the cat's limbs while the cat relaxes and makes no physical effort. Articulation takes this a stage further, and uses the cat's limbs as levers to stretch the soft tissues. In all techniques, the osteopath monitors the cat's response and makes adjustments to its treatment plan accordingly.

availability

Osteopathy is now recognized as a valid treatment for animals, although there are as yet no recognized schools of veterinary osteopathy. If you wish to have your cat treated osteopathically, it must first be examined by a vet. If the vet also thinks that treatment would be beneficial, a qualified human osteopath will work on your cat under the vet's direction.

It is important that the vet and the osteopath co-operate with each other. The vet's notes, diagnosis and schedule should be made available to the osteopath, and the osteopath should discuss the treatment, benefits and outcome. Failure to liaise effectively can result in an inappropriate treatment being given. Osteopaths may use other therapies in their treatment of human patients, but by law they are not allowed to use techniques other than osteopathy on your pet without the permission of the vet.

WHEN TO USE OSTEOPATHY

In the absence of scientific research it is difficult to evaluate the value of osteopathy in cats. However, where vets have referred cats for osteopathic treatment, the results have been encouraging. Osteopathy seems to be particularly useful to alleviate any joint pain arising as a result of road traffic accidents and degenerative diseases.

Although the theory of osteopathy is valid for all species, it is important to remember that cats, generally, do not like being handled by strangers. Their reluctance to co-operate with osteo-pathic treatment is a great drawback to its use, except when the cat is trusting enough to relax and allow manipulation, in which case good results can be obtained. However, if the cat refuses to co-operate, do not force it, but postpone the treatment session to another date. Alternatively, you may wish to consider a different therapy after discussing the options with your vet.

General osteopathic treatment

The initial stage of any osteopathic treatment is a total examination of the animal. The osteopath will work through a sequence of movements to manipulate the cat's limbs so as to identify a suspected misalignment. Note the gentleness of the techniques: this cat did not even need to be held.

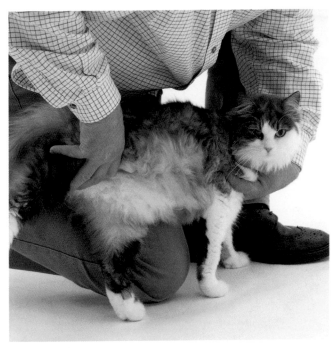

◁ **1** Examination and articulation of the cat's pelvic bones. Each hind leg is extended to stretch the muscles.

△ **2** Examination and articulation of the neck. The head is gently rotated clockwise to stretch the muscles in the neck and shoulder.

△ **3** Examination of the front leg. The cat lies on its side with its muscles relaxed, while the positions of the skeletal structure are examined.

▷ **4** Examination and articulation of the hind legs. The cat is lifted clear of the ground to extend the hind leg muscles and bone structure.

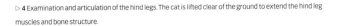

Physical therapies: chiropractic

Like osteopathy, chiropractic concentrates on the anatomy and physiology of the cat's musculoskeletal and nervous systems, and on the safe manipulation of the spine. The difference between the two therapies lies in their basic philosophy of disease.

what is chiropractic?

Chiropractic theory says that if vertebral segments of the spine are misaligned, there will be undue pressure on the spinal cord or spinal nerves. This can cause interference with nerve transmissions, which may result in abnormal function and disease. If the malfunctioning vertebral segment can be repositioned by manipulation, the pressure on the spinal nerve roots is relieved and normal nerve function is restored.

how it works

The first stage of chiropractic treatment with a human patient involves taking a detailed case history, and an examination of the nerves (neurological examination) and bones (orthopaedic examination). These same tests are carried out on a cat. The neurological examination includes reflex and nerve stretch testing; the orthopaedic examination tests the range of movement of the various regions of the spine. At the same time, positions that cause pain are noted, as are abnormal movements of the joints of the spine. The chiropractor will consult with a vet to take X-rays (radiography), which are used to check for the existence of spinal disease that might cause a similar clinical condition, and to rule out the possibility of serious spinal damage, such as fractures after recent accidents.

The chiropractor is concerned with the physical effect of restriction of movement of the spine, however small and subtle. A change in alignment of the surfaces of the small vertebral joints, together with an associated nerve dysfunction, is known as a subluxation, a term used to describe partial dislocations. Chiropractic diagnosis aims to recognize such restrictions and gives the appropriate treatment to adjust them. The adjustment itself seldom results in total correction but initiates the body's natural healing processes, which will complete the realignment. Chiropractic adjustment involves applying a high-velocity, short-amplitude thrust to the appropriate small facet joints of the vertebrae. It is the aim of the adjustment to correct the mechanical function of the joint and restore normal nerve function in the area.

Chiropractic is a non-invasive therapy, and while the hand movements are fast, they are subtle and extremely gentle. In severe or long-standing cases, chiropractic treatment may be given in a series of adjustments to give a gradual return to normal function, rather than in one or two more traumatic ones. Chiropractors are also taught deep-tissue massage techniques. These are used to support their manipulations, particularly in chronic cases. Drugs are never used in chiropractic treatment.

In spite of the difficulties involved with treating cats, chiropractic is a valid form of holistic treatment for cats who suffer the equivalent of back pain. Because drugs are not involved, the treatment is non-toxic. Adverse effects can occur after treatment,

▷ **Monitor your cat's response to treatment and stop treatment if the cat seems uncomfortable.**

although these cases are rare. Discuss the possibility of things getting worse before they get better with both the vet and the chiropractor before starting the treatment.

availability

In the United Kingdom, the McTimoney Chiropractic Association runs courses in chiropractic work on animals. The qualified practitioners treat animals referred to them by a vet. In the United States and Canada, the American Veterinary Chiropractic Association runs courses both for vets and human chiropractors who want to work on animals. Chiropractic treatment on animals is permitted by law only under the direction of a vet; only an animal-trained chiropractor is allowed to treat a cat. The practitioner is trained to handle different animals, but treating a cat can be made more difficult because of the cat's natural dislike of being examined. There should be good communication between the vet, the chiropractor and the owner.

WHEN TO USE CHIROPRACTIC

Chiropractic is not for home use. Because treatment involves manipulation of the spine, the consequences of misapplied techniques can be severe and could lead to paralysis. Even after observing the actions of a trained chiropractor during treatment sessions with your cat, never attempt to treat it yourself.

If you are having your cat treated, pay attention to its instinctive response to the practitioner. On subsequent visits to the clinic in particular, watch for any signs of reluctance, the need to escape, or defensive aggression. This may be your cat's way of telling you that it dislikes the treatment. No matter how beneficial you, your vet and/or chiropractor think the treatment can be for your cat, if the cat does not feel comfortable with what's happening, you need to put an end to the sessions and reassess the alternatives. Resentful cats cannot be treated successfully.

McTimoney chiropractic

The following sequence shows the checking procedure that is done before the problem can be diagnosed and treatment given. All types of ailments are treated by McTimoney Chiropractic, from strains and lameness to the animal's inability to move normally – for example, when running or jumping over a hurdle. Treatments can be given weekly or monthly until the problem has cleared. In general, six-monthly check-ups are advised after a course of treatment has been completed.

△ **1** The hands move along the cat's cervical and thoracic spine as the practitioner makes an adjustment to the thoracic vertebrae, which lies between the cat's shoulder blades.

△ **2** The practitioner positions the hind legs to check for subluxations in the pelvis area and the stifle (knee) joints.

◁ **3** Here, the McTimoney practitioner checks the thoracic spine. There is a chiropractic checking procedure for all animals. If a subluxation is located, the hand movements are adjusted accordingly.

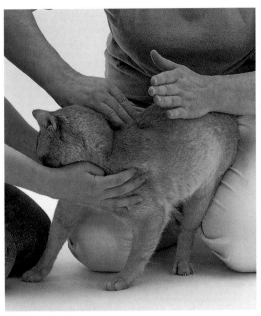

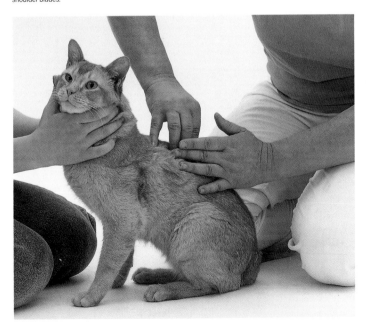

△ **4** The forelegs are then checked for signs of subluxations in the joints and elbows, which could be the cause of lameness.

Physical therapies: TTouch

The TTouch technique is very similar to massage, the difference being that it affects the skin only and not the underlying tissue. Gentle, rhythmic finger touches are applied to the cat's body to calm and relax it and to improve its capacity for training. TTouch is particularly useful for frightened cats.

what is TTouch?

The therapy was developed by a Canadian physiotherapist, Linda Tellington-Jones, who first worked with horses before extending her work to all other animals. Tellington-Jones developed her ideas from the work of Dr Moishe Feldenkrais, an Israeli writer who taught physical body awareness to humans. The theory is that non-habitual movements, combined with gentle manipulations, can promote body awareness, which in turn affects behaviour. The system is known as the Tellington-Jones Every Animal Method (TTEAM), and the individual strokes as TTouch.

how it works

The principle behind TTouch is that the skin is moved in a circular motion through just over 360 degrees. If you imagine a clock

△ The gentle TTouch movements can help where a cat's behaviour has deteriorated due to the stress and pain of an injury.

face on the skin, the movement is clockwise from 6 o'clock through 12 o'clock and 6 o'clock to the 8 o'clock position. TTouch stimulates the nervous system, and benefits the mental and emotional states. One effect of the technique is to change brain activity. Changes have been seen in the alpha, beta, delta and theta waves of horses.

Skin manipulation is done with one, two or three fingers, depending on the size of the cat. The thumb and the heel of the hand rest on the body, while the relaxed fingers move the skin. Only one circle is

made in any one position. The hand is then slid to an adjacent area of skin and another circle is made, with the sliding action connecting the two circles. Whilst one hand makes the circles, the other hand rests on the cat's skin for balance and to complete the connection between owner and cat.

There are 15 individual TTouch movements, each using different parts of the hand, and different pressures and speeds. The techniques include back and belly lifts, crossways movements across the belly, manipulation of the ears from base to tip (to stimulate the acupuncture points in the ear) and, if the cat will allow it, circles made in and around the mouth, lips and nose.

availability

You can practise TTouch on your cat at home. Light, flexible wands, or even feathers, can be used on cats that resent being touched. TTouch relaxes nervous animals, often allowing them to be handled safely in due course. It is a valuable technique for relaxing stressed or frightened cats that are in pain through injury. Regular sessions can also help to strengthen the bond that exists between owner and cat.

◁ Spending a quiet moment practising TTouch at home with a nervous cat can be hugely beneficial. Start with a single stroke and repeat it over the cat's body.

▷ You will gain the cat's trust quicker by paying close attention to its likes and dislikes as you build on your repertoire of strokes.

TTOUCH HAND MOVEMENTS

1 the clouded leopard

2 the lying leopard

3 the racoon

4 the snail's pace

5 the bear

6 feathering

7 the abalone

8 the lick of the cow's tongue

9 the tiger touch

10 Noah's march

11 the python lift

12 the butterfly

13 tarantulas pulling the plough

14 belly lifts

15 back lifts

The Leopard The "Clouded Leopard" is so called because of the light and stealthy hand contact; while the "Lying Leopard" uses a firmer pressure and a flatter hand position to give a more defined contact. The Leopard movements are used to focus an excitable cat.

The Racoon Use on cats for more delicate work; for working around wounds; to speed healing; to increase circulation and activate neural impulses in the lower legs; to reduce swelling without causing pain.

The Snail's Pace The slow contractions and extensions of the fingers are used to relax back and neck muscles, to improve breathing and to reduce stress.

The Bear For areas of heavy muscling, such as the shoulders, back and flank. The emphasis is on the fingernails making the contact, rather than the finger pads. The circle is made with the fingers pointing down, parting layers of muscle rather than digging into them.

Feathering For cats who are frightened of being touched, in place of the Bear. The movement should be light and fast.

The Abalone This mimics the slow circular motion of the sea abalone. It is not so much a movement as a firm, calming pressure that pushes the skin around the circle.

The Lick of the Cow's Tongue A gentle swiping movement upwards from the belly to the back to soothe and calm a nervous or anxious cat. On very sensitive animals, the skin may twitch. If this happens, stop the movement and make a light Abalone circle before moving on to the next area. This encourages calm breathing, and will discourage the cat from pulling away on contact.

The Tiger Touch A movement for physically strong cats, and for itch relief. The fingernails are the point of contact, and because the fingers are raised and apart, the nails almost make their own individual circles.

Noah's March Use these long, firm strokes to close a TTouch session: after the experience of revivification that the TTouch has brought to individual parts of the body, this will bring back a sense of wholeness. Using both hands, begin at the cat's head and make long, smooth strokes over the entire body.

The Python Lift Use on the shoulders, legs, neck and chest areas to relieve muscular tension and spasms. Place both hands on either side of the cat's body or leg and slowly lift upwards for 1–2 cm (½–1 in). Hold for 4 seconds, come back down, then slowly release. Lift just enough to support the muscle lightly; too much pressure may cause the cat to hold its breath.

The Butterfly Use this light movement alongside the Python Lift to increase circulation. The thumbs are pointed upwards with the fingers wrapped around the cat's leg. Lift the skin and muscle of the cat in the same way as for the Python Lift. Concentrate on moving slowly.

Tarantulas Pulling the Plough Use light, nimble movements to gently roll the skin, working in a smooth pathway across the cat's shoulders, back and sides.

Belly Lifts Start behind the front legs and lift the cat's abdomen. Hold for 10–15 seconds, depending on the reaction. It is important that the pressure is released slowly and takes more time than the lift. Move gradually along the body towards the flank and repeat. Go as close to the flank as is comfortable for the cat: some cats are very ticklish in this area, especially when in pain. Two people can work the movement holding a towel between them; one person working alone can use their forearms and hands.

Back Lifts With fingers apart and curved upwards, start on the far side of the belly in the middle. In a raking motion, bring both hands across the belly and partway up the barrel of the body. Start gently and increase the pressure if the animal doesn't respond. You should be able to see the top of the back rise upwards.

Like massage and TTouch, Reiki is a hands-on therapy. However, this technique also bridges the gap between the physical therapies and the energy therapies. Its hand-placements and movements on the surface of the body are designed to direct healing energy to an injured area and to strengthen the spirit, rather than to stimulate the skin and underlying tissues themselves.

what is Reiki?

The origins of Reiki are not certain. Some people believe that it was first used in India by the Buddha and, later, in the Middle East by Jesus. Its secrets were lost over the years but were more recently discovered by a Japanese doctor, Dr Mikao Usui. When the doctor was close to death from cholera, he joined a Zen monastery and was introduced to the theory of Reiki. In a vision, he was shown healing symbols from the holy texts (sutras) and was taught how to use them. He was also given the ritual of attunement which allows Reiki knowledge to pass from the initiated master to the uninitiated student. These rituals are still in use today.

The name Reiki is thought to originate from two Japanese symbols, "Rei" meaning universal and "Ki", the non-physical life-force. Ki is similar to the concept of Q'i

△ **The healing energy of Reiki can be used to heal a cat that is suffering an emotional upset.**

in acupuncture, and the vital force of homeopathy. Ki is a powerful healing energy and is available to anyone who can learn how to use it. The pressures of modern life mean that most of us are disconnected from Ki. Reiki aims to reconnect people to this universal life-force, giving them the capacity to heal themselves, their families, their friends and their pets.

◁ **Reiki hand placements channel the healing energy to where it is best absorbed. The cat's chakra at the sides of its face is very receptive to the positive life-force.**

SOME HAND POSITIONS FOR TREATING CATS

Choose one of the following to give your cat the benefit of a Reiki treatment at home whenever it is needed. If your cat is suffering physical or emotional distress, be sensitive to its response; if the cat shows signs of resentment, stop the treatment immediately. For cats suffering recent physical injury, do not place your hands directly on areas of acute inflammation, but hold your hands parallel to, and just above, the damaged area, so as to be able to focus the healing energy where it is needed.

- With the cat seated on your lap or on the floor in front of you, hold your hands on either side of the cat's ribcage. This will treat the cat's whole body and the Reiki will reach the central parts immediately.
- Put one hand on the head of your cat as though you are going to stroke its ears, and one hand very lightly on the middle of the cat's back.
- Hold the cat between your hands, with one hand at the top of the spine and the other at the base, by its tail.

how it works

There are three degrees of Reiki. In the first, the student is attuned to the life-force and can begin to channel the healing energy where it is needed. The student is taught the hand placements and move-ments that are needed to direct the energy to the patient. In the second degree, the student is taught the symbols and healing sounds (mantras) that focus the energy on the patient. The student is also taught how to use Reiki for distant healing. The third degree, or Reiki Master level, is the teaching level. The knowledge of this degree is passed from master to student during a private, sacred ceremony.

▷ Giving the cat a whole body treatment will direct the flow of energy where it is needed. Start with your hands over the bud chakra at the base of the cat's ears and work towards the feet.

using Reiki

Reiki energy is a universal life-force that connects all life forms, and it can be used to treat animals in the same way as humans. Reiki can provide an uplifting tonic or pick-me-up, or it can ease physical pain and suffering. It can also be used to reassure cats who are emotionally upset.

When treating an injured cat, place your hands parallel to and above the wound. The cat will move away or will appear restless when it has received enough of the healing energy.

It is not recommended to use Reiki as the only method of treating a sick animal. If your cat is injured or appears to be ill, consult the vet as normal, then use Reiki as a support to any prescribed treatment. The best use of Reiki is preventative, to help keep your cat in a state of good health and to prevent serious disease from becoming established.

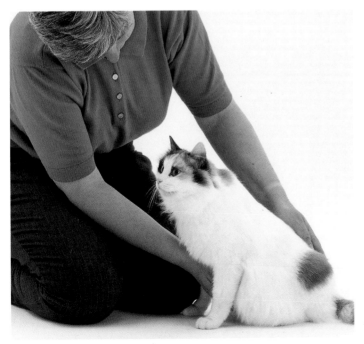

△ If the cat is suffering acute pain, move slowly and with relaxed movements. The cat will usually let you know when it has had enough.

◁ Reiki can be used on an unwell cat to support conventional veterinary treatment, and can help to soothe physical or emotional pain.

Medicinal therapies: herbalism

Medicine is the art of restoring and preserving health using remedial substances and dietary regulation. It is also the name given to the substance used in this art, which is usually taken internally. Medical substances fall into three categories: herbals, which are simple plant extracts; synthetic drugs, which are produced commercially by the pharmaceutical industry; and volatile plant oils, which are used in aromatherapy.

what is herbalism?

This is probably the oldest form of healing still in use today. Herbal medicines play an essential part in both Traditional Chinese Medicine (TCM) and the Indian Ayurvedic system. Western herbalism dates back to the ancient Greeks. It was the mainstay of English medicine until the early 1930s, when the group of medicines

◁ **Standardized commercial extracts will have a more constant effect than home-made teas.**

known as sulphonamides, the precursors of modern antibiotics, were first introduced.

Herbalism is now making a resurgence, caused in part by an increasing suspicion that the long-term effects of some modern drugs may not be totally beneficial to the patient. This suspicion is prompting a reappraisal of all medical therapies and is encouraging an interest in holistic medicine and a desire for effective natural treatments, for both humans and animals, which do not involve toxins or side effects. The fact that cats and other animals actively seek out and eat plants that are known to have medicinal properties supports the view that herbalism should have an established and widespread place in orthodox veterinary medicine.

Many people take the view that, almost by definition, natural is synonymous with safe. As herbal medicines are natural, they must therefore be safer than manufactured ones. This is not necessarily the case and herbal medicines should be treated with the same respect as pharmaceutical drugs. Some plants are poisonous in their natural form and herbal medicines derived from an original plant source can be toxic if given in too high a dose. Always check the toxicity of your chosen plant.

Some pharmacists object to the use of herbalism on the grounds that the chemical

marshmallow

△ **Preparations of marshmallow root soothe the bowel lining and can be useful in cases of chronic vomiting, diarrhoea and colitis.**

composition of individual plants of the same species may vary according to the soil they are grown in and the time of the year they are harvested. This means that medicines derived from plants cannot be standardized, unlike manufactured drugs. This is compounded according to which part of the plant is used and the method of extraction. Pharmacists would prefer to isolate the part of the plant that they consider to be the active ingredient, and use only that ingredient in a purified form. This is the only way to know in advance exactly what effect a single dose of medicine will have on the body.

Unfortunately, few active agents have only one effect. They also tend to have other unwanted actions or side effects. Herbalists believe that the active ingredients of herbal medicines work together to counteract harmful side effects. This allows a safe, effective dosage to be made.

WHEN TO USE HERBALISM

Condition	Herbal therapy
Cancer protection	barberry bark; comfrey leaf; echinacea root; fenugreek seed; lemon balm; mistletoe leaf; Roman chamomile flower
Diarrhoea	garlic; marshmallow root; slippery elm bark
Itchy skin	burdock root; fenugreek seed; German chamomile flower; liquorice root
Liver disease	barberry; dandelion milk thistle
Kidney problems	cleavers; goldenrod; parsley
Skin abrasions	comfrey leaf; peppermint; turmeric root; yarrow
Urinary tract disorders	bearberry leaf; couch grass; cranberry; field horsetail; juniper berry; marshmallow root

▷ Diluted eyebright tincture can be used to bathe inflamed eyes, while diluted calendula lotion can be used on mild infections.

using herbalism

Herbal medicines can be administered in many ways. The traditional method is in the form of herbal infusions or teas, which are made from bulk herbs sold loose by weight. Like all herbal preparations, bulk herbs should always be purchased from reputable firms. Herbal teas for cats are made in the same way as they are for humans, with hot water poured over herbs in a tea strainer. The difference seems to be that cats appear to need more than humans in relation to their body weight. A dose of 15 ml (3 tsp) twice a day is accepted as suitable for a cat weighing 5 kg (11 lb). Good-tasting bulk herbs can be fed directly to the cat if mixed with its food.

Commercial herbal extracts in the form of glycerine/water and alcohol/water tinctures are also available, and these can be

▽ Suspicious cats may be willing to take commercial extracts if they are added to favourite foods.

given directly into the mouth, if your cat will tolerate it. Here, the dose rate is one drop per 1 kg (2¼ lb) of body weight. Herbal capsules and tablets are available for cats, but some authorities believe that capsules of powdered herbs are not suitable for carnivorous animals. If using these, follow the instructions carefully. Bulk herbs can also be used to make poultices and compresses. Do not use toxic herbs in this way as a cat may lick the dressing and poison itself.

There are very few practising veterinary herbalists. Some vets undertake courses in

herbalism to combine it with scientific knowledge. When treating animals, the vet will monitor the response to treatment and will amend the dose accordingly. As experience of veterinary herbalism grows, so dosing regimes become more accurate.

In cases of minor illness, you can treat your cat at home. Keep up the treatment for one week before rejecting it, if it seems to be ineffective. It can take longer to see improvements in chronic cases, although in these situations, herbalism is best used to support conventional care. If ever the cat's condition appears to deteriorate at all, stop the treatment and consult your vet.

Medicinal therapies: aromatherapy

Aromatherapy is the use of volatile aromatic oils, which are derived from plant material, to cause physiological and psychological changes in the patient. The molecules of these essential oils are able to enter the body and the bloodstream by absorption either through the lining of the nose and lungs, or through the skin. This means that essential oils used for aromatherapy should always be handled with care and the same respect as any other medicinal substance.

essential oils

Fragrant essential oils have been used medicinally in Egypt and the Middle East for thousands of years. Their use is not taught in medical or veterinary schools at the present time, although many holistic veterinary clinics employ qualified aroma-therapists, as do some human hospitals.

Several parts of the plant are used as a source of the essential oil. Flowers, leaves, twigs, roots, seeds, bark and heartwood may all be used, depending on the plant. There are several methods of extracting the oils, the commonest being steam-distillation. This yields an oil and water mix that is cooled and separated into its two components. Pressing is used to squeeze the oil out of plants containing non-volatile oils. Carbon dioxide extraction can also be used

but is more expensive. Enfleurage is the traditional method of oil production, and involves laying petals on layers of fat for up to three weeks. During this time, the oils seep into the fat, from which they are then separated by extraction with alcohol. This method is used for extracting delicate flower oils, such as rose and jasmine. It produces fine quality oils which are very expensive. Solvent extraction produces oils known as absolutes, which may contain traces of the solvent. For this reason they are disliked by some therapists. Synthetic oils are also produced. Although these are a standardized product, they are unlikely to contain as many components as the natural oil, and this may reduce their therapeutic effect. Some aromatherapists believe the reason synthetic oils are not as active as the natural oils is because they have an artificially produced chemical source, which is devoid of the vitality of living materials.

There are hundreds of component oils in every extract of essential oil. The final contents are governed by the geographical area and the soil in which the plant is grown, the climate, and the methods used in cultivation. Some people prefer those oils produced from organically grown plants, as this eliminates any contamination with

lavender

◁ Lavender oil is non-toxic but should never be used on damaged skin.

agrochemicals. Whichever type of essential oil you choose, always buy from a reputable supplier; regard cheap oils with suspicion, but bear in mind, too, that expense does not necessarily indicate quality.

using aromatherapy

Cats have a highly developed sense of smell, providing it has not been reduced by cat flu or similar diseases. Cats use the secretions of their anal sacs, and the glands in their cheeks and tails, along with saliva, urine and faeces, as a means of communication and to mark their territorial boundaries. Because their

◁ All essential oils should be blended with a carrier oil if they are to be used for massage on a cat. Essential oils containing phenolic oils should never be used on cats.

◁ Essential oils should not be rubbed into the cat's fur. If they must be rubbed in, dilute 2 drops of the essential oil in 15 ml (1 tbsp) of a vegetable-based oil, and use the bald areas of the groin and armpit.

sense of smell is so refined, most cats will respond well to aromatherapy. However, you should never force your cat if it appears unwilling to co-operate.

Essential oils are not to be taken internally by cats because of the risk of toxicity. For the same reason, it is not advised to massage a cat with oils because of the absorbency of the skin. Baths are obviously unsuitable for animals. The most effective way of using aromatherapy with your cat is in a diffuser. In this method, 5–10 drops of oil are floated on water which is heated by a candle; electric vaporizers are also available. The heat will cause the oil/water mixture to evaporate, and the fragrant vapour fills the room, where it is inhaled by everyone, people and pets alike. This is ideal for home.

Essential oils are chosen according to the cat's symptoms. Combinations of up to four oils can be burned at one time, and blends for use in a vaporizer can be prepared at home. Essential oils are concentrated chemicals and can be highly toxic in their neat form: never use them undiluted on an animal's skin. A cat will try to clean the oil off and may ingest toxic amounts by doing so. Remember, too, that a cat's nose is very sensitive. What smells beautiful to you may be unbearably strong for your cat, and if so, the treatment will not work.

Aromatherapy can be used to support any mainstream or complementary therapy with the exception of homeopathy, because homeopathic remedies can be deactivated by highly aromatic substances.

WHEN TO USE AROMATHERAPY

Condition	Essential oil
Lack of confidence, anxiety, panic	sandalwood; ylang-ylang
Loneliness, fear of being alone	basil; bergamot; orange blossom
Restlessness, frustration	chamomile
Liver problems	rosemary
Kidney and bladder problems	juniper
Skin allergies	lavender; pine; terebinth
Respiratory problems	cedarwood; eucalyptus; lemon; tea-tree
Minor skin wounds, bites and stings	lavender; tea-tree
Toothache	clove

△ Vaporizers are efficient but they should only be placed where they cannot be overturned.

Medicinal therapies: pharmaceuticals

Even when adopting a holistic approach to health, conventional Western medicine has its place. Acupuncture, herbalism and homeopathy are complete systems of medicine in their own right, but this does not necessarily mean that these systems are equally effective 100 per cent of the time. Each individual is unique, with their own particular response to treatment. Every cat will respond in a different way to the same treatment. Complementary treatments can and do work, and sometimes they will effect a complete cure. There are also times, however, when modern medicines are needed, forming part of an approach using a well-chosen combination of several therapies.

what are pharmaceuticals?

Many modern medicines are derived by isolating the active ingredient found in herbal medicines. Having isolated and identified the chemical structure of the active ingredient, attempts are then made to synthesize medicines that have a similar structure and a stronger action. These tend to have more pronounced side effects as well. The first antibiotic, penicillin, was isolated from a fungal culture. Since then, other natural antibiotics have been found, and synthetics based on the chemical structure of the natural products have been manufactured. However, the side effects of synthetic drugs usually become more serious as new generations of antibiotics are developed. Scientists have also manufactured synthetic hormones and vitamins, but some of these are less effective than the natural product.

how they work

Modern Western medicine is based on an accurate diagnosis. After the illness has been correctly identified and named, the aim is to find and administer the one, true medicine which will cure the condition. This is the magic bullet to kill the disease. It is a beautiful idea but medicines have more than one, simple action in the body. Unwanted actions are the side effects of the drug. When medicines are given in short courses of small doses, the body is able to correct any damage which may have been done, inadvertently, by the medicine whilst it heals the disease it was sent to cure. In chronic disease, where medicines are given over long periods of time, the side effects can overcome the body's ability to deal with them. The original natural disease is now worsened by medicine-induced disease. It might be argued that chronic disease is itself an indication that medicine has not brought about a cure but has simply suppressed the original symptoms, giving a false impression of a cure.

when to use pharmaceuticals

Modern medicine is at its best in cases where the cat has a mineral or hormonal deficiency. Injections or tablets will replace the missing nutrient or hormone, although dietary changes will be needed to prevent a recurrence. For example, in diabetes, which is becoming increasingly common in cats, replacement of the necessary hormone with insulin injections will correct the deficiency and restore normal glucose metabolism. Properly supported by an appropriate complementary therapy, the amount of insulin needed can be reduced, and sometimes the need for replacement therapy disappears altogether.

In acute bacterial infections, antibiotics are very useful, but good complementary medicine, used alongside the drugs, will often allow the use of shorter courses of antibiotics than would otherwise be needed. Such a holistic approach will reduce the number and the severity of the side effects experienced by the cat. It will speed convalescence and correct the weakness that allowed the infection to occur in the first place. Steroids are useful when your cat has a severe inflammatory condition (they

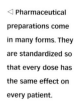

◁ **Pharmaceutical preparations come in many forms. They are standardized so that every dose has the same effect on every patient.**

▷ If you tickle your cat's throat when giving tablets or medicine, it will encourage the cat to swallow.

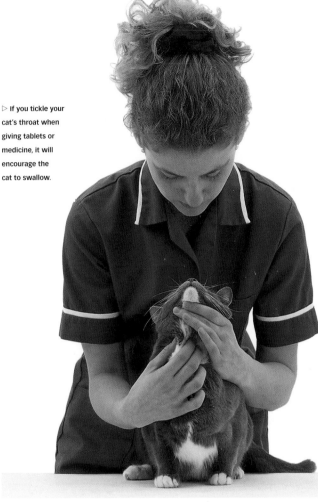

△ Hold your cat's eyes open with gentle pressure of your thumb and forefinger, so that you can put drops in accurately.

△ Hold the cheekbones with one hand, tilt the head back and pull down gently on the jaw: the cat's mouth will then open.

should only ever be used in short courses) but good complementary support used alongside antibiotics can provide similar benefits without the need for steroids. With certain cancers, chemotherapy is a valid treatment, although its extremely painful and distressing side effects can be reduced if a sensible holistic treatment plan is used in support.

Modern medicine has a genuine place in the treatment of disease. Ideally, however, it should form just one part of a holistic approach to your cat's health.

▷ Injections are given into the muscles of the front of the thigh to avoid the nerves and blood vessels, which are situated towards the back.

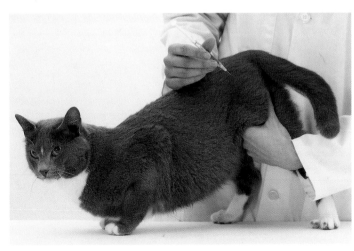

Energy therapies: acupuncture

Acupuncture forms part of Traditional Chinese Medicine (TCM), which was first developed by the Chinese over 3,000 years ago and is still practised today.

what is acupuncture?

Acupuncture is based on a principle of the flow of energy, or Q'i (pronounced chee), around the body through non-anatomical channels known as meridians. If the flow of Q'i passing through any of the channels is disturbed, the health of the body will be impaired, which leads to disease.

The body's energy flow increases and decreases in each meridian in a fixed cycle. The meridians also govern the function of anatomical units, although their function in TCM is different to Western medicine.

Q'i has two opposite, complementary components: yin and yang. Everything in the universe contains yin and yang, but some things contain more yin than yang and vice versa. The solid organs of the body – liver, spleen, kidney, heart, lungs and pericardium – are yin, while the hollow organs – stomach, small and large intestines, gall bladder and urinary bladder – are yang. One pair of meridians governs each organ, and there are two other non-paired meridians, the Governing Vessel and the

Conception Vessel. These meridians run in pathways up the front and down the back of the body.

Acupuncture theory states that everything in the universe is made from five basic philosophical elements: wood, fire, earth, metal and water. These elements relate in a positive or negative way to one another, so that wood produces fire, but restrains or destroys earth. Each element can change to the next in the course of a creative cycle.

Chinese acupuncture recognizes six environmental factors as the reasons for disease: wind, cold, summer heat, dampness, dryness and heat; each is associated with certain forms of disease. It also recognizes eight conditions composed of four pairs of opposites: yin and yang, heat and cold, internal and external, excess and deficiency. The theory is that disease can be expressed by a combination of these eight conditions.

how it works

No medicines are given, although Chinese herbs may be used to support treatment. Treatment is by the stimulation of precise anatomical points on the meridians; the knowledge of these points is based on results recorded over thousands of years.

Today, fine surgical steel needles are inserted into underlying tissue. The relationships between the elements, environmental factors and conditions of opposites indicate which points on which meridian should bring Q'i back into balance and allow the body's own healing forces to complete the cure.

There is no anatomical structure or organ recognized by Western medicine that is penetrated by the needles and which could be responsible for the physical and physiological changes that can result from treatment. The effects of acupuncture cannot be explained in either physical or biochemical terms, which suggests

△ Fine surgical steel needles have replaced the slivers of bamboo or bone that were first used in acupuncture to stimulate the meridian points.

CONDITIONS THAT BEST RESPOND TO ACUPUNCTURE
- Back pain and paralysis from injury and disc problems
- Conditions: allergies and dermatitis; epilepsy; non-spinal origin paralysis; chronic gastro-intestinal conditions, such as diarrhoea or vomiting
- Respiratory diseases and asthma
- Painful neuralgic type conditions and general pain relief

that they occur at a different level, in the invisible, energetic bodies that surround the physical body. For many conventional, Western-trained physicians, acupuncture and its approach to treatment is hard to evaluate. A form of acupuncture has been developed in the West which uses fixed combinations of points for each diagnosis. It is empirical, but the essential art of TCM has been lost. Western acupuncture cannot be used on as many conditions and the results are inferior. References in this book are to Chinese acupuncture.

treatment for cats

Q'i, the philosophical elements, the environmental factors and the conditions of acupuncture are universal, which means that acupuncture can be used as easily on animals as on humans. The position of the meridians and acupuncture points varies from species to species, but the techniques are just the same. Your cat will not tolerate over-stimulation and will always let the practitioner know when it has had enough.

Acupuncture is not as effective as antibiotics at treating acute infections, but it is very good with chronic diseases, including diseases of the immune system.

This therapy is not for home use: the untrained use of needles can be dangerous. Your vet will refer you to a practitioner if you are interested in using it on your cat.

◁ A thorough clinical examination of the cat should be made, and a Western diagnosis given, before a course of acupuncture is begun.

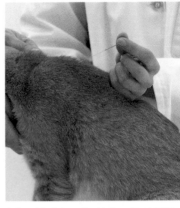

△ The points that are stimulated are chosen on the basis of the examination, the cat's case history and the experience of the practitioner.

acupressure

By law, only qualified vets are allowed to use acupuncture needles on animals. However, if you wish to provide back-up care for your cat, simple training from a qualified practitioner will allow you to perform finger pressure, or acupressure, at home in support of any conventional treatments your cat may be having.

Like acupuncture, acupressure is based on the theory of Q'i, and is said to reduce pain by relaxing the muscles. It is applied with very light fingertip or finger-nail pressure on the acupuncture points; some styles of acupressure also involve rubbing, kneading and rolling. Acupressure done incorrectly can increase pain. As with any therapy, do not continue if your cat appears to resent the treatment.

△ Cats will usually tolerate acupuncture reasonably well when they are ill, but they will always let you know when they have had enough.

◁ The cat's acupuncturist can show you the correct acupressure points so that treatment can continue at home.

Energy therapies: homeopathy

Homeopathy was the first holistic system of Western medicine to be developed. It can be very effective both on its own and in support of conventional medicine and, like acupuncture, it is at its best where conventional medicine is weakest.

what is homeopathy?

The body has a natural healing force, which comes to the fore in cases of ill health: minor cuts and grazes heal on their own, and we quickly recover from mild coughs and colds. Science calls the healing force homeostasis, and homeopaths believe that their medicine stimulates it.

Samuel Hahnemann, an 18th-century German doctor and the originator of homeopathy, called the body's basic impulse towards self-healing the Vital Force. He saw it as an energetically active, living force, which is essential to life. From his observations he deduced that a non-lethal quantity of a poison can stimulate healing of any disease where the symptoms are similar to the effects of that poison.

The idea that like cures like dates back to the ancient Greeks, but had never before been used as the basis for a medical therapy. Hahnemann tested his substances on himself and his friends, and recorded the results in a volume he called the *Materia Medica*.

Hahnemann used small, material doses, and noted that some patients got worse before they got better, a phenomenon he called homeopathic aggravation. To lessen the aggravations he reduced the dose, but although dilution made the aggravations less severe, it also lessened the benefits. Next, liquid medicines were shaken after dilution in a method known as potentizing. This reduced the aggravations while, at the same time, it enhanced the healing property of the medicines, or potencies.

The use of highly diluted medicines has led to two main misconceptions. First, that the essence of homeopathy is the use of a very small dose rather than the use of a "similar". Second, that because there are no molecules left in the highly-diluted potencies (above *24X* or *12C*) the medicine could not possibly work. However, observations over the last 200 years have shown that these medicines do affect the living body. The phenomenon is under scientific study, but the method by which homeopathy achieves results will probably prove to be at a sub-atomic level. Homeopathy is as relevant to animals as it is to humans.

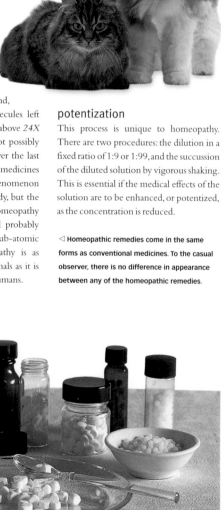

▷ **The gentle action of homeopathic remedies works well in cats.**

potentization

This process is unique to homeopathy. There are two procedures: the dilution in a fixed ratio of 1:9 or 1:99, and the succussion of the diluted solution by vigorous shaking. This is essential if the medical effects of the solution are to be enhanced, or potentized, as the concentration is reduced.

◁ **Homeopathic remedies come in the same forms as conventional medicines. To the casual observer, there is no difference in appearance between any of the homeopathic remedies.**

WHEN TO USE HOMEOPATHY

Remedies are available in different potencies, of which the most common are *6C* and *30C*.
Use *6C* for chronic or long-standing conditions, and *30C* for emergencies and acute conditions.

Condition	Remedy
Panic attacks and sudden emotional stress	Aconite
Prolonged grief, bereavement	Natrum mur.
Flea bites and insect stings	Apis mel.
Bruising and other trauma	Arnica
Flatulence and digestive disorders	Carbo veg.
Skin grazes and superficial wounds	Hypericum; Calendula
Physical exhaustion	Arnica

WHEN TO USE TISSUE SALTS

Condition	Remedy
Neurological disorders	Kali phos.
Allergies	Nat. sulph.
Chronic infections	Silica
Dental problems	Calc. fluor.

The starting point of any potency is the saturated solution of a soluble chemical, or the alcoholic extract of plant material, known as the mother tincture. Each succeeding potency is given a number for the number of dilutions made, and a letter for the Latin number of the degree of dilution, *X* or *D* standing for 10, *C* for 100 and *LM* for 50,000. For example, if you put one drop of the mother tincture of *Belladonna* with 99 drops of alcohol/water and succuss it, you get a *1C* potency. One drop of the *1C* potency mixed with 99 drops of alcohol/water gives a *2C* potency, and one drop of a *2C* potency mixed with 99 drops of alcohol/water gives a *3C* potency, and so on. Potencies up to *30C* are still made by hand, and to these is added the suffix H for Hahnemann. Potencies from *30C* to *10M* are usually produced by mechanical methods.

homeopathic treatment

A similar is the medical agent which produces symptoms closely resembling those of the cat; if the symptoms match completely, it is a similimum. When a cat is treated, its physical, mental and emotional reactions to the world are used to identify the disease. The totality of the animal and its condition is treated, and the more you know about your cat when it is healthy, the more you can help when it is ill. The

▷ **If you experience difficulty in giving your cat a homeopathic tablet, it can be crushed and mixed in with the cat's food.**

smallest dose of the similimum that will stimulate the healing process is given. In acute cases, doses are repeated until benefits are seen. In chronic cases, each dose is left to have its full effect before it is repeated.

The second branch of homeopathy is the removal of obstructions to a cure. This relates to the holistic idea that unless there are suitable nutrition and lifestyle changes, a permanent cure cannot result.

Tissue salts make up the third branch of homeopathy. In the 19th century, a German homeopathic doctor, Wilhelm Schüssler, identified 12 basic salts present in the body. He thought that all diseases, if caught early, and without complex symptoms, could be cured by the correct combination of these salts. Biochemic tissue salts are prescribed in a low, *6X* potency to alleviate mild disease or emotional conditions, which may be caused by a mineral salt deficiency. Nutritional advice will usually be given as part of the treatment.

Energy therapies: Bach flowers

Plants and flowers play an essential part in many traditional healing systems. The Bach Flower remedies, prepared from the stalks, petals and leaves of plants, can be used to treat mental and emotional states.

what are flower remedies?

The 18th-century German homeopath, Dr Samuel Hahnemann, used the vibrational energy of plants to stimulate natural healing processes in his holistic system of homeopathy. A British bacteriologist, Dr Edward Bach, took Hahnemann's ideas one stage further. His experience as a homeopathic doctor had convinced him that physical disease was the body's reaction to a non-material cause. Changes in the body's fundamental vibrational energy (an acupuncturist's Q'i and a homeopath's Vital Force) resulted in a pathological change of mental state that could eventually lead to physical disease.

To Dr Bach, mental attitude was more important than physical symptoms when choosing a medicine. He believed that the mind showed the onset and cause of disease before the body. In 1930 he set out to seek a means of healing that used non-toxic materials rather than potentized poisons.

rose

⊲ **The wild rose flower remedy can put a spring in the step of lethargic cats.**

Dr Bach was a sensitive, spiritual man who noted that his own moods could be strongly influenced by the plants he came into contact with. He looked to individual plants for his remedies, and his theory was that the natural vibrations of certain plants seemed to match the vibrations associated with certain mental states. Therefore, if these plants were appropriately prepared, they may be able to help correct distorted vibrations by the principle of resonance.

Bach intuitively discovered 12 plants which could affect pathological mental states. He later increased the range to 37 plants, and added *Rock Water*, which is water from a natural spring (preferably one reputed to have healing properties). He also sanctioned the use of a combination of five remedies in a preparation he called *Rescue Remedy*. *Rescue Remedy* is the most popular, general-purpose Bach Flower remedy for both humans and animals. It is best used in emergency situations as a calming treatment for all types of panic, shock and hysteria.

▷ **The boiling method is used to provide the mother tincture of those plants that bloom in winter or the early spring.**

⊲ Dr Bach's remedies covered all the emotional states of his era. More remedies have been developed in recent years to cope with modern life.

traditional preparation

Bach chose two methods of preparation for his plants, based on seasonal availability. Flowers that bloomed in the late spring and summer were picked at 9 a.m. on sunny days. The flowers were floated on 300 ml (½ pint) of spring water in a glass bowl and left in sunlight. If the sun clouded over, the batch would be discarded. The flowers were removed using stems of the same flower so that the energized water was not

contaminated by human touch. The ener-gized water was used to fill bottles half-full of brandy. This was the mother tincture. Two drops of this added to 30 ml (2 tbsp) of brandy gave the stock solution.

Plants that bloom in the late winter and spring were prepared by the boiling method. Flowers and stems were picked on sunny mornings. They were collected in a pan, and when the pan was nearly full, the lid was fitted and the material was taken home. The flowers and stems were covered with 1.2 litres (2 pints) of spring water and simmered for 30 minutes, uncovered. The lid was then replaced and the covered pot put outside to cool. When cool, the stems were removed, and the liquid filtered and used to make the mother tincture, as before.

The plants used in the remedies should be wild ones, growing in unpolluted areas. If cultivated plants are used, they should be organic and free from any chemical contamination. *Rock Water* should also be free from agrochemicals. Flowers from several plants are used.

Stock solutions of single Bach flower remedies are now sold ready-prepared, in health food stores and large chemists (drug stores). These remedies may be given alone or combined with up to five essences at a time to make a medicine. To prepare a medicine, add two drops of each essence to 30 ml (2 tbsp) of spring water.

◁ Bach flower remedies are taken in a very dilute form. Two drops of stock solution make 30 ml (2 tsp) of medicine, which is diluted further when taken.

using flower remedies

Flower remedies are particularly valuable for emotional problems and, while clinical tests have proved inconclusive in explaining how and why they work, positive results have been seen in humans and animals. Choose the remedies according to the cat's mental state, using human emotions as a guide. The cat's temperament is the key, so the better you know your cat, the more you can help it. Treatment is based on the usual temperament and not on the nature of its inappropriate behaviour. The simplest way to treat your cat is to add 3–4 drops of essence to its drinking water.

Dr Bach believed his remedies covered all known emotional states, and it probably is true that they addressed the most widespread symptoms of his era. More recently, however, other series of flower essences have been developed, such as Californian and Australian Bush flower remedies. These have been developed with modern life in mind, and offer treatments for such factors as the ill effects of pollution and stress. These remedies are prepared and used in the same way as the Bach Flowers, and although they can be used on cats, they are perhaps less relevant for animals than for humans.

WHEN TO USE BACH FLOWERS

State of Mind	Flower Remedy
Shyness	Mimulus
Apathy	Wild Rose
Hormonal imbalances	Scleranthus
Lack of self-confidence	Larch
Maliciousness	Willow
Aloofness	Water Violet
Excessive desire for company	Heather
Possessiveness	Chicory
Dominance	Vine

▷ Flower essences can be added to the cat's drinking water to help treat emotional problems.

Energy therapies: crystal therapies

Crystals have been used for healing purposes for thousands of years. Empirical studies indicate that through harmonic resonance, the vibrational energy of a crystal can affect the basic energetic vibration of both humans and animals.

what is crystal therapy?

Crystals have a fixed, atomic structure, as opposed to the chaotic arrangement of atoms in non-crystalline material. The natural energy of the atoms is harmonized by this structure and every crystal has a natural frequency of vibration.

The energy of the crystal is believed to enter the body through the chakras of Indian Ayurvedic medicine. Each chakra is related to a hormone-producing gland in the body, and each has its own harmonic colour vibration. In turn, these correspond to seven layers or energy bands in the aura – the invisible energy field surrounding the physical body. Because of the universality of life-energy, these factors are as valid for animals as they are for humans. The only difference is the location of the chakras within the physical body. They have

citrine

◁ **Yellow stones relate to the chakra that governs the nervous, digestive and immune systems. Stress, fear and happiness are all linked to this colour.**

amber

iron pyrites

tiger's eye

tiger's eye

rutilated quartz

been accurately mapped in humans, but the corresponding chakras are not identical for animals. There is some controversy over the location of the minor and bud chakras in cats, although there is general agreement about the major chakras.

using crystals

As with Bach Flower remedies, the mental state of the patient is the major factor in choosing which crystals to use. Some crystals have an affinity for certain body systems or symptoms. The factors quoted for crystal selection for humans can be applied to cats and other animals.

Once the appropriate crystals have been selected, they are placed on the patient's resting body in set patterns. For a cat, the crystals can be taped to its collar or an improvised harness if the cat will tolerate it. It is also possible to use liquefied crystal essences, which are produced in a similar way to the flower essences and can be successfully used to treat both mental and emotional problems.

Crystals can also be used in light therapy. Light is shone through coloured crystal filters in a darkened room on to the cat's body; the light is directed either on to a chakra, acupuncture point, or the region of the affected organ. Colours have long been known to affect the human mind and this phenomenon is used when choosing

THE CHAKRA SYSTEM FOR CATS

Crown/brow (major)

Ears (bud)

Solar plexus (major)

Root (major or minor)

Nose (bud)

Throat (bud)

Belly or Belly/root (major)

Tail tip (minor)

Paws (minor)

△ **The vibrations of crystals can restore balance to a cat's energy field. Every crystal has a vibrational rate which governs its therapeutic use.**

△ If the cat will lie still, the appropriate crystals may be placed near the relevant chakra rather than using harnesses. This may be a preferable treatment method for some less tolerant cats.

colour schemes for high-stress areas such as hospitals and police cells. It may be that animals are similarly affected by colour.

Crystal healing is helpful for cats whose illness is due to mental and emotional problems, and it can be used to support all physical and medical therapies. Do not use crystal therapy on unset broken bones, or before surgery, as it can interfere with the anaesthetic. Discuss crystal therapy with your vet before treatment is started and only proceed with the vet's approval.

how crystals work

Crystals contain metallic ions which can benefit the body's metabolic system. These are slowly absorbed by the body through the skin, if the crystal is placed in contact with it. This is similar to the use of essential oils in aromatherapy.

It has been demonstrated that if a human holds a crystal in the hand for more than 30 minutes, the brain waves change from the alert beta waves to the more relaxed alpha waves. The deep relaxation pattern associated with theta and delta waves will increase if the crystals are held for periods of more than half an hour.

While crystals emanate positive healing vibrations, they also absorb negative and pain vibrations from the patient. To maintain the healing potential of crystals it is necessary to cleanse them regularly. They can be left outside for a 24-hour period when the moon is above the horizon: it is said that the dual action of sunlight and moonlight over this period will cleanse the crystal.

Alternatively, the crystal can be left to stand in salt-water for 24 hours and then taken out of the water and left, pointing downwards, for eight hours to dry. Iron-containing crystals can be cleansed using spring water in the same way. Porous crystals, such as lapis lazuli and moonstone, should not be washed. These should be buried outside in the ground for 24 hours and then wiped clean with a paper towel, using a little spring water, if necessary, to remove all traces of dirt.

CHOOSING CRYSTALS

Amethyst	a healing stone to calm the mind
Bloodstone	to heal and energize the physical body
Blue lace agate	a cooling, calming stone to lighten thought
Citrine quartz	an energizing stone, physically and mentally
Clear quartz	for general well-being
Lapis lazuli	releases stress to focus and calm
Moonstone	clears tension from the emotions and abdomen
Rose quartz	to balance the emotions
Smoky quartz	a grounding stone and a deep cleanser
Tiger's eye	a stable and stimulating energy

blue lace agate

amethyst

tiger's eye

Holistic Cat Care

Look in the perfumes of flowers and

nature for peace of mind and joy of life.

From the writings of Wang Wei, 8th century

Treating your cat

Cats can bring us great pleasure when we keep them as pets. In return, it is up to us to make sure that they are properly looked after, and that if they become ill, they receive the best possible treatment.

who can treat your cat

As the cat's owner, by law you have the right to treat minor ailments yourself, but serious conditions can only be treated by, or under the supervision of, a vet once the cat has been examined and a diagnosis made.

Only a vet is qualified to prescribe medical drugs. Likewise, the practice of treatments such as acupuncture, chiropractic and osteopathy must be left to animal-trained therapists. The borderline case is herbalism. Using proprietary medicines available from chemists (drug stores), Western herbalism can be used at home. On the other hand, herbalism that forms part of Traditional Chinese medicine (TCM) is only for qualified practitioners. If you are ever in any doubt about holistic treatment, consult your vet.

using home treatments

If your cat is showing signs of being mildly unwell, some of the therapies discussed in this book can be used at home with a basic self-taught knowledge of the therapy.

If you are interested in holistic treatment for your cat, it might be worth taking an introductory course in the therapy which most appeals to you. Veterinary courses are available in TTeam, TTouch, homeopathy and the Bach Flower remedies. It is more difficult to find animal-based courses for crystal therapy, massage or Reiki. One of the good things about holistic therapies, though, is that they are energetically rather than anatomically based, and the species of the patient does not seem to matter. It is possible to adapt knowledge of the therapy as it applies to humans over to cats – providing you use a little common sense.

Mood swings, emotional distresses, or early signs of behavioural problems can all be treated in the first instance at home. Similarly, if the cat has only mild physical symptoms, such as diarrhoea and vomiting, a cough or muscular stiffness, you can try the therapy of your choice. When the cat is in severe pain, has blood in any of its bodily discharges, or if it does not respond to home treatment, you should see a vet. Similarly, if your cat suffers from the same minor symptoms again and again, you should consult your vet, who will check for a more serious, underlying cause. This is one of the reasons why conventional medicine is such a necessary part of holistic care.

a supportive role

If your cat is seriously ill, holistic therapies may be used in a supportive role alongside conventional treatment, with the vet's agreement. Medical conditions, such as diabetes, will often respond quickly to conventional veterinary treatment. The correct use of complementary medicines, however, can reduce the amount of drugs needed, and may even give a complete cure. Similarly, after surgery, holistic support can help to speed up the recovery.

working together

The veterinary profession the world over is beginning to take an increasing interest in holistic medicine, but as yet few vets have much experience of using it. The next time you visit the vet, tell him or her of your interest. Ask what the prescribed treatment is designed to do and, if there are any side effects, if there is a complementary therapy that would help your cat. Let the vet know that you want to work together for the benefit of the cat – it is extremely important that conventional and holistic medicines are used in a complementary way. In the end, the aim of both is to make sure the animal enjoys a long and happy life.

◁ Massage is one of the simplest ways to help your cat at home. You don't need equipment or training, just an understanding of your cat.

△ Cats do not all appreciate being dosed with medicine or manipulated by strangers, so consider your cat's usual likes and dislikes when choosing a therapy. Both the homeopathic and the Bach Flower remedies are tasteless and easy to administer. The close contact involved in the massage therapies will strengthen the owner-cat bond. Holistic therapies are equally effective in cats of all breeds and all ages. They can help to extend the active life of a cat, allowing it to enjoy all of the quiet spaces of the natural world.

Behavioural problems: house-training

The inappropriate elimination of urine and faeces is the commonest behavioural problem in cats, and the one most likely to create difficulties for its owner.

Kittens are still very young when they develop their preference about where to eliminate their waste. Problems with this will arise because of one of three situations: in the adoption of an untrained (usually feral) cat, when a trained cat suddenly loses its house-training, and when the cat starts to deliberately use its urine and faeces as a means of marking out its territory.

If you decide to take in a feral cat, the normal house-training routine should be started immediately. Put the cat on to the litter tray or outside after meals, and when it looks as if it wants to go. Try different substances in the tray until you find one that the cat finds acceptable. Remember also that cats are very private animals and that its tray should be well away from the busy part of the house, its eating utensils and its sleeping area. If there are other cats in the home, it may be necessary to provide separate trays for each cat. Close-confining a cat with a litter tray may speed things up but it can be so stressful to a cat that has been used to free-roaming, that the stress can outweigh the benefits.

Sometimes a cat that has always had clean habits will start to mess in the house; this behaviour may have physical and/or mental

▷ Cats are very private creatures and dislike being disturbed when using the litter tray. Keep its tray in a quiet area of the house to give the cat privacy.

origins. If a cat has a bowel or urinary tract infection, it may be unable to control itself long enough to get to a tray or outside. If this happens often enough, the cat may persist with inappropriate elimination even when it gets over the infection. If the cat has started to habitually use another part of the house, that area should be cleaned with an enzymatic odour-removing product. These are available from veterinary surgeries and good pet shops. A second tray can be placed in that area on several thicknesses of paper, on top of a layer of thick polythene to

prevent any soiling going through to the floor covering. Alternatively, the cat and a suitable litter tray can be kept in a small room – usually the bathroom – to encourage it to use the tray. Cats are very particular, and many dislike reusing a soiled tray, so regular cleaning is a good idea.

Mental and emotional causes, however, are probably the most usual reasons for a loss of house-training. Fear is a frequent cause of loss of training. The most common fear is of being attacked by another cat or a dog that has moved into your cat's territory. If the cat has been involved in a road accident, this can also deter it from going outside. Fear can also develop if the cat associates using its tray with an unpleasant experience, such as accidentally having things dropped on it, being attacked by the family dog, or being disturbed by very loud noises, such as smoke alarms and children's noisy toys, for example.

complementary treatment

If you think that fear may be the underlying cause of your cat's distress, use the Bach Flowers *Mimulus*, *Cherry Plum* and *Rock*

◁ The Bach Flower remedies can help in cases where a loss of house-training is the result of an emotional disturbance of some kind.

Rose to support a retraining plan, or try the homeopathic remedy *Aconite*. Give TTouch to help reassure the cat, and the aromatic oils *Basil*, *Chamomile* and *Lavender* can be used in a diffuser. If you want to try these oils in a massage, dilute 2 drops of oil first in 15 ml (1 tbsp) of a vegetable-based carrier oil. Use an oil massage no more than once or twice a week. Herbal infusions of *Chamomile* or *Vervain* can help; the tissue salt *Mag phos.* may act as a nerve tonic.

Feelings of resentment closely follow those of fear. Resentment can happen when a foreign cat comes into the house, eats your cat's food and uses its litter tray. Or it could arise when your cat has been sent away to a cattery or when a new pet or baby comes into the home. In such cases, try the Bach Flowers: *Centaury* for lack of assertiveness, *Elm* for feelings of inadequacy, or *Willow* if the cat is showing concurrent destructive behaviour out of spite, perhaps

◁ **Covered trays such as this are favoured by the more timid cat. The top is removable to facilitate cleaning.**

to pay you back for being sent away from home or ignored. Homeopathic *Staphysagria 30C* can be given twice daily for resentment, and herbal infusions of *Passiflora* and *Vervain* may also help. TTouch will help to restore the cat's confidence.

The extreme case of territory marking by spraying or defecating in the house, will often be done as a response to an outside threat, as above. When a cat sprays to mark its territory it aims at a vertical surface

◁ **Make sure that the tray is large enough for your cat, and that it contains a litter of your cat's liking.**

30–45 cm (12–18 in) from the floor. It does not squat in the way that it does when it urinates. Try the Bach Flower *Rescue Remedy* and homeopathic *Staphysagria*. If circumstances permit, it's also a good idea to treat the invading cat, using the Bach Flower *Vine* or the homeopathic remedy *Lachesis*. If the aggressor is an exceptionally strong bully, homeopathic *Platinum 30C* given twice daily for five days may help. If your cat is an un-neutered tom who is spraying, then it is most likely due to hyper-sexual behaviour. In such a case, the homeopathic remedy *Ustilago maydis* may be of some help.

If your cat does not show any sign of improvement in its house-training, or if the behaviour seems to get worse, you should see the vet, who will check for signs of physical abnormality or disease. He will either prescribe treatment or, in the absence of any disease, he may suggest pheromone sprays to put around the house on the furniture and walls to inhibit spraying. The vet may also prescribe anxiety-reducing (anxiolytic) drugs for the cat. A referral to a behavioural specialist may be suggested in particularly stubborn cases.

Behavioural problems: aggression

Aggression in cats is not usually a serious problem for their owners, and cats rarely need to be referred to animal behaviourists for treatment.

Cats may still show isolated signs of aggression towards other cats and/or humans. Inter-cat aggression, as its name suggests, is shown only to other cats; assertion or status-related aggression is shown only to humans. There are many other types of aggressive behaviour which are shown towards both cats and humans.

▷ Cats have no "natural handles". The scruff of the neck probably gives the safest hold on a cat of uncertain temperament.

inter-cat aggression

The classic, violent cat fight usually occurs between two toms wanting to mate with the same queen. This is the most common example of inter-cat aggression. To reduce the likelihood of your tom being involved in too many fights, he is best neutered before he is six months old. This will control his testosterone levels, which may otherwise cause him to fight. The other treatment is to keep him shut away from other cats, except when he is needed for stud purposes.

Inter-cat aggression is not restricted to tom cats, however. It can also be male-to-female and female-to-female, particularly in households with three or more cats. The dominant cat will take up an aggressive stance and the other will try to defuse the situation and avoid physical injury, its body language suggesting a deferential pose.

It is only when two cats feel of equal status that the trouble starts. In this case, the cats have to be housed in separate rooms, the more aggressive cat being given the smaller, less attractive room. When their owner is present, however, the cats can be

in the same room. If the dominant cat shows aggressive behaviour it should be startled, using a rattle or horn, and gently moved back into isolation. If there are no signs of aggression, give both cats a treat.

When the cats can be in the same room without fighting, they can be brought closer together using harnesses and given treats as rewards for good behaviour. Try feeding the cats in the same room but with their food bowls well apart, gradually bringing them closer together over a period of time. The dominant cat can be treated with homeopathic *Platinum* or *Lachesis*, or the Bach Flower *Vine*, whilst homeopathic *Staphysagria*, or the Bach Flowers *Centaury* and *Elm* are for the submissive cat. T Touch given to both cats can help the situation; herbal infusions of *Passiflora* and *Vervain* can also be given to the inferior cat.

◁ When fighting breaks out regularly, treat both cats. Try to subdue the dominant cat whilst strengthening the weaker one.

causes of aggression

Lack of socialization with humans arises when kittens have not had enough human contact in the first 7-10 weeks of life. These cats tend to grow up displaying aggressive behaviour towards humans and are difficult to treat. Not interfering with the cat is usually the best approach to take. The Bach Flowers *Beech* or *Rock Rose* can be tried, as can homeopathic *Stramonium* for fear of being attacked. TTouch, using a wand, can be helpful. The burning of the essential oils *Sandalwood* and *Ylang-ylang* has also helped in some cases.

When a cat is in a situation of perceived danger and it cannot escape, it is likely to become aggressive through fear. Recognize that the cat is frightened and under stress;

do not advance, but back off and give the cat its chance to run away. TTouch is good, as are the Bach Flowers *Aspen*, *Cherry Plum* and *Mimulus*, and *Stramonium* can be tried. If these do not help, the vet may prescribe a tranquillizer. If the situation is recurring, refer your cat to a behaviourist.

Aggression may be caused by pain resulting from disease, accidents, surgery or a course of painful injections. In such cases, the cat needs sensitive handling, while its pain can be treated with homeopathic *Arnica*; an appropriate Bach Flower remedy can be used for emotional disturbance.

THE CAT'S MAJOR FACIAL EXPRESSIONS

calm: face relaxed, teeth covered, ears pricked

worried: ears back, pupils dilated with fear

ready to attack: ears back, eyes narrowed

reconsidering attack: ears back, eyes widened

warning: ears back, eyes narrowed, teeth shown

ready to attack: ears down, mouth open, teeth bared

THE CAT'S MAJOR TAIL POSITIONS

calm

affectionate

enthusiastic

defensive

submissive

stalking prey

COMPLEMENTARY TREATMENT

TTouch is good for calming anxious cats. Wands may be necessary for safety reasons. This can be tried on rehomed cats and kittens that are not properly socialized to humans. Aromatherapy, using the essential oils of *Sandalwood* and *Ylang-ylang* can be helpful if used in a diffuser. Herbal preparations can be helpful. Infusions of *Chamomilla* relax cats that become angry and bite from impatience. The proprietary *Skullcap* and *Valerian* tablets have a calming effect. Bach Flower remedies can be successful where negative emotional states cause aggression. They may be used singly or in combinations of up to five essences. If pain is causing the cat to bite, *Star of Bethlehem*, *Sweet Chestnut* or *Rescue Remedy* can be given. Homeopathic remedies should be given singly, using a *30C* potency twice daily for up to five days. They should be reduced or stopped if an improvement is seen. If there is no improvement, consult a homeopath: some remedies are developed for specific situations. *Belladonna* helps cats that explode with anger; *Nux vom.* helps those that are irritable, sensitive to noise and have bowel troubles. Crystal therapy, using liquid-gem oral remedies, can modify behaviour by stabilizing the emotions.

Behavioural problems: pining

Ask any cat-owner and they will almost certainly be able to think of a time when their cat showed signs of upset after being left or sent away. Cats are more emotional creatures than many people think.

Pining is a form of separation anxiety, mixed with sadness or resentment. It is commonly seen in cats whose owners have died, but it can also show itself when the cat is put in the cattery, if it has to be rehomed, or when its greatest friend leaves home. Typical signs of bereavement in the cat are a loss of interest in life and a withdrawal into itself. This may progress to a loss of appetite and thirst. It has been known for cats to starve and dehydrate themselves so badly when put in quarantine or even in a cattery, that intravenous feeding was needed to keep them alive until they could go home. Treatment with vitamins and anabolic steroids does not stimulate the appetite of these cats.

Resentment can appear as physical symptoms. In extreme cases, the cat's coat becomes greasy, clumps form in the fur, and the skin is scurfy. The skin of the belly and groin may also become dry, red and itchy, with flakes of scurf around the neck. Some cats develop incontinence and/or cystitis, and may have blood in their urine.

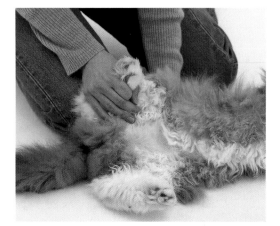

◁ **Massage with the essential oils of basil, bergamot and orange blossom, diluted in a vegetable-based oil, on the bald groin area can help to relieve emotional stress.**

▽ **Large flakes of scurf around the neck can indicate resentment and the need for the homeopathic remedy, staphysagria.**

Orthodox treatment for both skin and bladder problems is with antibiotics and steroids. However, if these problems are emotionally based, then the treatment is rarely successful. Typically, there will be an initial positive response to treatment which then slips back, and a chronic condition will often become established. Complementary therapies, which tackle the underlying emotional problem, are more effective in producing a permanent cure in these cases. Conventional and holistic therapies can also be used together.

COMPLEMENTARY TREATMENT

TTouch can be given both at home and in a cattery to help the cat feel loved. Aromatherapy with *Basil*, *Bergamot* and *Orange Blossom* can all be useful and you can try the Bach Flowers: *Heather* for loneliness, *Honeysuckle* for homesickness, and *Walnut* to help the cat adjust to the change in its circumstances. Homeopathic *Ignatia* is used for the mood-swing type of grief, whilst *Natrum mur.* is used when the coat is greasy and there is a loss of fur that starts at the base of the tail and works its way back towards the head, a bit like an arrowhead. Resentment that shows itself by a loss of house-training, cystitis (possibly with blood in the urine), or a dry red itchy skin that begins in the belly and groin region, can be helped by homeopathic *Staphysagria*. Young kittens are likely to miss their mother when first rehomed. They can be given the Bach Flower remedy *Honeysuckle* for their homesickness. If the stress is so great as to cause physical illness like diarrhoea, the homeopathic remedy *Capiscum* may help.

△ **Greasy fur with dandruff at the base of the tail is often the first sign of separation anxiety. Homeopathic natrum mur. will often help to acclimatize the cat to its new situation.**

Behavioural problems: destructiveness

Destructiveness in the house usually takes the form of scratching at the furniture. Carpets, doors and soft-furnishings can also be favourite scratching places. If left unchecked, the scratching can eventually cause unsightly and expensive damage to items around the home.

Cats like to scratch solid objects for two reasons: as part of a grooming routine and as a way of marking their territory. In grooming, cats often develop a preference for a particular type of material. Cats which are allowed to roam outdoors will mark their territory with secretions from the glands between their toes, as well as with the visual signs of their scratch and nail shreds. Outdoors, cats have access to many types of materials and this reduces their need to scratch indoors. These cats are not likely to cause problems until they become elderly, when they spend less and less time outside and may start looking for suitable objects to scratch at indoors.

Cats kept entirely indoors need a scratching post of some kind. Most cats prefer a vertical surface, about 1 m (1 yd) high, which will give them a good stretch as they scratch. These poles may be covered by thick sisal rope or carpet, or they may

◁ The use of nail clippers will reduce the damage caused to furniture as the cat uses its foot glands to mark its territory.

△ A finer nail file or emery board can be used to trim the nails of kittens and younger cats.

be left bare. Young kittens can sometimes be trained to scratch on a specific surface by gently dragging their toes and nails over the material, particularly if this is introduced as part of a nail-cutting session.

The need to scratch can be controlled if the cat can be persuaded to let you trim its claws regularly, using clippers or a nail file. This should be started early in its life to accustom it to having its feet handled. When clipping claws, you may find it easier for both of you if you turn the foot backwards to expose the under-surface of the foot, in the same way as a blacksmith does when lifting a horse's hoof.

Destructiveness in the house can also take the form of territorial marking, as exhibited by scratching and/or spraying. If your cat is an only one, then this will not usually be a problem. However, if a second cat is introduced into the household, it can prompt the first cat into an orgy of scratching and spraying as it asserts its right to control the whole house.

The second cat does not even need to be a member of the household to cause problems. A dominant cat may have moved into the area, and be trying to take over not

only your cat's territory, but also its house, feeding bowl and litter tray. This will cause your cat to mark inside its home with even more enthusiasm. You can discourage the intruder by using a startler rattle, water pistol or similar whenever you see it. At the same time, try startling your own cat if you see it about to mark indoors. Your vet can prescribe a pheromone furniture spray, which will further deter your cat.

COMPLEMENTARY TREATMENT
You can encourage your cat to stand up for itself by using the Bach Flowers *Centaury* for submissiveness, and *Walnut* to help the cat to adjust to new circumstances. Use the home-opathic remedy *Staphysagria* if the cat seems resentful and *Colocynth* if it is angry. Give reassurance and support with TTouch. The essential oil of *Chamomile*, used in a vaporizer, will help to relieve the cat's anxiety and calm it down.

Behavioural problems: jealousy

Jealousy is an emotional state that many scientists believe only exists in human beings. However, there are indications that cats are also subject to this emotion. In a jealous state, the cat will become over-conscious of its rights and privileges and tries to retain them if it considers them to be under attack. These rights extend to territory, food and people.

The arrival of another cat, the birth of a baby, or even the presence of a friend or partner are situations in which the owner's attention is diverted away from the cat, triggering it into jealous behaviour.

If a kitten is introduced into the house it may seem to get on well with the existing cat. Well-adjusted cats will partition their home with invisible boundaries and each animal will have its own share of the house without too much fuss. Trouble may not start until the younger newcomer attains social maturity at about two years old.

Following the birth of a child, some cats can take a dislike to the new baby. If jealousy is suspected, it is wise to keep the cat away from the child, and to pay as much attention as is practical to the cat, to make it feel it is still loved and part of the home.

Where adults are concerned, cats may try to push their way between their owner and a close friend or partner. Some cats will attempt to drive the other adult away by force, and others will try attention-seeking behaviour, such as continuous vocalization

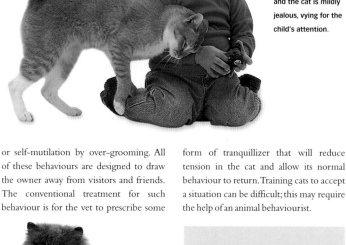

◁ Cats and young children usually get along well together. However, this child is immersed in his toy, and the cat is mildly jealous, vying for the child's attention.

or self-mutilation by over-grooming. All of these behaviours are designed to draw the owner away from visitors and friends. The conventional treatment for such behaviour is for the vet to prescribe some

form of tranquillizer that will reduce tension in the cat and allow its normal behaviour to return. Training cats to accept a situation can be difficult; this may require the help of an animal behaviourist.

△ Jealously can lead to the cat trying to draw attention to itself by displays of bad behaviour.

◁ Complementary treatment is more rewarding than chemical sedation when the problem gets out of hand.

COMPLEMENTARY TREATMENT

Give regular TTouch sessions to restore confidence and balance to a disturbed cat. Aromatherapy diffusions with *Ylang-ylang* and *Sandalwood* essential oils can also help to make cats feel more secure in the home. The Bach Flowers can be tried: *Chicory* for a possessive cat, *Red Chestnut* for being overprotective, and *Vine* for territorial aggression. Use homeopathic *Lachesis* for aggressively jealous cats, and *Pulsatilla* for the normally gentle cat who has a tendency to push and nudge between humans to claim its rightful place. *Pulsatilla* is particularly appropri-ate if the cat produces bland, yellow discharges and suffers any infection, particularly of the eyes and/or nose.

Physical problems: the eyes

Perhaps one of the most striking features of a cat is its eyes. In a healthy cat, these are clear and bright and can vary in colour enormously – beautiful shades of amber, green or blue are all common. The pupil should be black; its shape varies according to the light conditions: in bright light it narrows to a slit, but as it gets darker the pupil becomes rounder and larger. At times of extreme fear, the pupils dilate and the iris almost disappears.

Although a cat can see extremely well in the dark, it takes at least half an hour for its eyes to adapt to a sudden loss of light. In the wild this does not matter, but a cat leaving a well-lit house at night will effectively be blind for a while whilst its eyes adjust. This may account for the fact that most of the road traffic accidents involving cats take place shortly after the cat has gone outside at night.

It is a good idea to check your cat's eyes as part of its daily grooming routine. The condition of the eyes is a good indication of the cat's overall state of health.

discharges and inflammation

Cats have a third eyelid that moves across the surface of the eye, from the inside corner towards the outside. The third eye is clear and membranous, and under normal circumstances it is barely visible. However, if the eye looks painful, or if the pad of fat on which it rests disappears, this membrane becomes more obvious. If it comes into view and remains visible for more than 48 hours – even if there is no sign of inflammation or discharge – consult the vet in case it is the first sign of a more serious disease.

Any discharges from the eyes should be noted as these can occur for several reasons, some minor and some more serious.

△ **Regular cleaning of eye discharges, particularly in the long-haired breeds, helps to keep the facial fur free of unsightly stains.**

The tear duct is responsible for draining tears into the nose. If this becomes blocked or is absent for any reason, it may result in a mild tear overspill on to the face. Tear duct problems are more common in the flat-face breeds, such as Persians. If the discharge is mild, the eye can be cleansed with warm salt-water or a cold tea solution. If the problem persists, your vet can check to see if the tear duct is working properly. If it isn't, the cat may need a small operation to clear the duct under a general anaesthetic.

Thick purulent discharges from the eyes are generally more serious. These may be a sign of cat flu, or that a foreign body, such as a grass awn, may have worked its way behind the third eyelid and become stuck in the eye.

conjunctivitis

The conjunctiva is the peachy-pink membrane that lines the lids and surrounds the white of the cat's eye. An inflamed conjunctiva is known as conjunctivitis. If there is inflammation but no discharge,

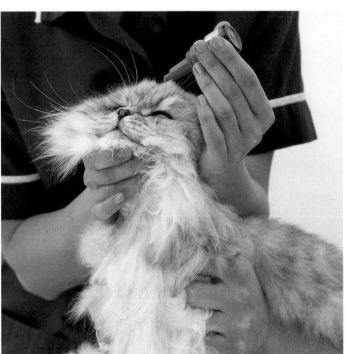

◁ **Many cats resent being treated. An extra pair of hands is often needed to get drops into the eyes of an unco-operative animal.**

▷ Diluted euphrasia tincture, or a herbal infusion of golden seal, will soothe inflamed eyes. Apply with a soaked wad of clean cotton gauze or cotton wool (cotton balls).

you can try bathing the eye with a solution of homeopathic *Euphrasia* tincture diluted 1:10 with water, or a herbal infusion of *Golden Seal*. Homeopathic *Apis mel.* may be indicated if the eye is red, the conjunctiva very swollen and there is marked weeping of the eye. This can be given every two hours. If the cat shows no improvement after six hours, you should contact the vet.

If the conjunctivitis is accompanied by discharges, the eyes can be bathed as above, and the following homeopathic remedies may be tried: *Arsen. alb. 6C* if the discharge is watery and scalding the fur off the cat's face, *Kali bich.* if the discharge is thick, green and stringy, or *Pulsatilla* for a mild and gentle cat with a creamy yellow discharge.

If the symptoms don't improve in 36 hours, or if the condition keeps recurring, the cat should be checked for a more serious underlying condition. If none is found, a homeopathically-trained vet may prescribe a constitutional

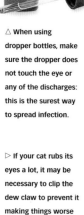

△ When using dropper bottles, make sure the dropper does not touch the eye or any of the discharges: this is the surest way to spread infection.

▷ If your cat rubs its eyes a lot, it may be necessary to clip the dew claw to prevent it making things worse by inadvertently scratching the eye.

remedy to help your cat. Alternatively, try to improve the cat's resistance to infection, using *Ferrum phos.* in the absence of discharges, *Kali mur.* for white discharges, or *Natrum phos.* for sticky yellow ones.

corneal ulcers and glaucoma

The delicate, transparent part of the eyeball is known as the cornea. It is frequently damaged in fights, but grass awns and other foreign bodies can also scratch the eye. Left untreated, scratches can develop into corneal ulcers. As these deepen, the cornea can burst and the eyeball loses its fluid and collapses. Sight is then permanently lost in that eye.

If you suspect your cat has damage to its cornea, it should be seen urgently by a vet, who will test the eye for ulcers. If ulcers are found, you can support the vet's treatment by bathing the cat's eye with *Golden Seal* or diluted *Euphrasia* and the following homeopathic remedies: *Argent. nit. 6C* if the cat is anxious; *Acid nit. 6C* if it is irritable or aggressive; *Merc. cor. 6C* if the eye is very sore, the cat dislikes the light and the discharge is greenish; and *Kali bich.* in the unusual case where the eye is painless. *Silica 30C* can be given when treatment is already underway, to help with the final stages of healing.

Sometimes the iris, or even the whole of the eyeball, can become infected, usually as a result of a deep infection after a bite. In such a case, the cat must be seen by a vet immediately. You can support the prescribed conventional treatment plan with homeopathic *Hepar sulph. 30C* and infusions of *Greater Celandine* to bathe the eye and to soothe it.

Infection and damage to the eye's inner structures can result in a build-up of fluid within the eye. The eyeball becomes swollen and red, and the cornea turns a cloudy white colour, with a red fringe around the edge. This condition is known as glaucoma and is extremely painful and serious. It can lead to damage of the retina, loss of vision and, sometimes, to a loss of the eye itself.

If you suspect your cat has glaucoma, it should be taken to the vet immediately. The vet's treatment can be supported by bathing with *Euphrasia* and trying homeopathic remedies: *Phosphorus* for the very active, demonstrative cat who is afraid of thunder, and *Spigelia* if the eye is extremely painful. Begin by giving the appropriate remedy hourly and reduce the frequency when you see signs of improvement.

cataracts

If you notice any white spots in the cat's pupil it may be an early indication of cataracts. These spots can grow to make the entire pupil look a milky-white colour and the clear lens of the eye becomes cloudy. These opacities prevent light from reaching the retina (the light-sensitive tissue at the back of the eye) and cause blurred or partial loss of vision. Eventually they may lead to a total loss of sight.

△ **Euphrasia, otherwise known as eyebright, is used as both herbal infusions or as a diluted homeopathic tincture for sore eyes.**

Cats can be born with cataracts (congenital) or they may develop later in life as a result of poisoning, ageing or the effects of diabetes. If you suspect your cat has cataracts, you should seek your vet's advice immediately.

Unlike the more traditional surgical methods, which need the cataract to grow to a certain size before it can be cut out, laser surgery techniques can be used very successfully to treat cataracts at a very early stage.

The main drawback of laser surgery is that it can be expensive and may not be appropriate in every case. If laser surgery is unavailable, bathe the eye twice daily with the homeopathic *Cineraria* tincture diluted 1:10 with water. This needs to be kept up for several months. Alternatively, it can help if the cat's eyes are bathed with a fresh herbal infusion of *Greater Celandine*. This can be supported with the tissue salts *Natrum mur.* for cataracts in their early stages, or *Silica* for long-standing cases.

In addition, the following homeopathic remedies can be tried: *Calc. carb. 6C* for overweight cats, *Phosphorus 6C* for thin, nervous cats, and Silica for naturally large-bodied cats with thin legs.

The diet can also be supplemented with a daily dose of 100 I. U. of Vitamin E (d-alpha tocopherol) in the form of wheatgerm oil, and a daily tablet of Selenium 25 mg, as these are claimed to slow the growth rate of cataracts.

A blow to the cat's eye, such as from a road accident or from a thrown stone, can be helped with homeopathic *Symphytum*, when there is marked pain but little bruising, and *Ledum,* when the bruising is severe, even to the point where there has been bleeding into the front chamber of the eye. *Ledum* is also recommended when the cat's eye has been punctured by a sharp object, such as another cat's claw, but there has been little or no fluid lost from the eye.

▽ **Tablets of Vitamin E can be given if wheatgerm oil is not readily taken. The taste of the tablets is usually acceptable to the cat.**

Physical problems: the ears

Ear problems in cats fall into either one of two categories. Either they arise as a result of a problem with the metabolism, or else they are the result of infections following bites to the head during cat fights.

The ear canal is lined with glands that produce natural wax in controlled amounts in a healthy cat. These glands are also capable of excreting mineral salts and other toxins if these are allowed to build up excessively in the body. Excess abnormal secretion, however, changes the micro-climate within the ear canal, which then allows unfriendly bacteria and parasitic insects to live and flourish in the ear. The presence of these organisms can cause unnatural and foul-smelling discharges. Similar changes in micro-climate also occur when foreign bodies, usually grass awns, find their way into the ear.

There are two things to check when examining your cat's ears: their colour and their smell. A healthy cat's ears should be a light pink colour on the inside. Some cats, however, have white, unpigmented ear flaps and are prone to developing cancer of the ear. This can be prevented by the use of a sunblock when there is bright sunlight. If the edge of the flap becomes crusty and thickened, see a vet straight away as surgery may be necessary.

Your cat's ears should smell clean and healthy, with very little odour. If the ear

◁ Sunblock can be used to help prevent bright sunlight causing cancer of the ear flap in cats with white ears.

starts to smell it is a sign of infection. The Indian herbal cream *Canador* is useful in the early stages, and *Echinacea 6X* will help to detoxify the cat and support its immune system. Before the infected stage really takes hold, try cleaning with the homeopathic remedy, *Hypercal* tincture, diluted 1:10 with water. Alternatively, two drops of lemon juice in 5 ml (1 tsp) of water, or a mixture of three parts *Rosemary* infusion added to one part of witch-hazel lotion can be used to clean wax from the ear. If you know your cat's homeopathic constitutional remedy, a dose should help with the underlying cause of the problem.

A dark, dry, crumbly wax usually points to the presence of otodectic mites. In this case, it is worth trying a mixture of one part each of *Rosemary*, *Rue* and *Thyme* mixed with three parts of olive oil to clean the ear.

If an offensive smell or discharge starts, or if there is no improvement in five days, then you should take your cat to the vet. Depending on the case he may give an antibiotic and steroid drops, or else he may suggest a general anaesthetic so that he can clean the ear and search for any grass awns.

Both of these measures can be supported with holistic treatments. Homeopathic *Graphites 6C* can be given four times a day

rosemary

◁ Regular rosemary infusions can help get rid of ear mites.

◁ A mixture of rosemary, rue and thyme diluted with olive oil is better than rosemary alone when there is a lot of wax present in the ear.

◁ Emotional issues can underlie chronic ear infections as well as behavioural problems. Advice from an aromatherapist may be helpful.

can be applied to the ear flap. Sometimes *Pulsatilla 6C* is better for gentle affectionate cats and *Phosphorus* often works in cats that hate thunder. The tissue salt *Ferrum phos.* can be given for a few weeks if the problem has a tendency to recur.

middle and inner ear infections

If your cat has an ear infection, it must be treated. If infections are neglected, they can spread to the deeper parts of the ear. If this has happened, there will most likely be an awful discharge and the cat may start tilting its head to the affected side to compensate. Untreated ear infections can eventually lead to loss of balance.

These cases will all need vigorous orthodox treatment, but referral to a homeopathic vet will result in the treatment of any underlying causes. Any nutritional imbalances and/or stress factors would also be addressed. Emotional problems can be supported by the Bach Flower remedies, or possibly by aromatherapy, if homeo-pathy is not available.

△ Homeopathic hamamelis is useful for injuries like haematomas which are painful and where there is passive venous bleeding.

if the discharge is very sticky (similar to glue ear in children) and *Hepar sulph. 30C* every two hours if the ear is hot, painful and sensitive, reducing the frequency as the ear improves. *Sulphur 30C* and *Psorinum 30C* can be given twice daily for up to three days to help the internal disturbance. Use the former on itchy cats that like to be cool, and the latter on itchy cats that hog the fire. Cats that need these remedies are usually dirty and scruffy-looking.

If grass awns are removed from the ear, diluted *Hypercal* tincture will be sufficient, or else an infusion of *Thyme* can be used to bathe the ear.

aural haematoma

If your cat is a fighter, it runs the danger of breaking the tiny blood vessels in its ear. The cat's ear flap is essentially a bag of skin, attached to an inner sheet of cartilage. The blood vessels of the ear lie on the inner side of the cartilage. If these vessels bleed, the blood fills and distends the bag to produce a swelling known as a haematoma – the same injury sustained by boxers when they get cauliflower ears.

The conventional treatment consists of cutting the inner surface of the ear, draining

the blood clots and then sewing it up like a mattress so that it can't swell up as it heals. An alternative method is to drain the blood through a wide-bore needle and then inject a small amount of a steroid into the ear through the same needle. This procedure sometimes has to be repeated two or three times before it is successful.

If the haematoma is caught in the early stages, homeopathic *Arnica 6C*, given four times a day for two days, may stop the bleeding, and *Hamamelis 12C*, twice daily, may help to reverse the process. *Hamamelis* cream or lotion

▷ Cats' ears are often injured during fights. The majority of such injuries do need conventional treatment but holistic support will greatly help the cat during recovery.

holistic cat care

Nasal problems are very common in cats, the most likely cause being infection, either from one of the cat flu viruses, organisms such as chlamydia, or bacteria.

cat flu

Vaccination gives some protection against cat flu but it does not always give 100 per cent immunity. Many cats are then left with a fairly continuous snuffle, or a snuffle that reappears when the cat is stressed, as is often the case when it goes into a cattery.

The discharges of cat flu are usually thick and purulent, and interfere with the cat's sense of smell and its breathing. There is usually a lot of sneezing, accompanied by a loss of appetite and thirst. Since the infections are mainly viral, antibiotics are not a satisfactory solution: they can only prevent secondary bacterial infections and

△ It is important that the cat's nose is kept clean. Cats find mouth breathing difficult, and the loss of smell causes a loss of appetite.

cannot kill the virus. Instead, the virus has to run its course and the cat may need intravenous fluids and nourishment to help it survive. The inflammation can also spread to the trachea and cause coughing.

Complementary therapies can be very successful with both the acute and chronic forms of cat flu. Homeopathic *Natrum mur.* is useful if the discharge looks like egg white, the skin is greasy and the flu started in the cattery. *Pulsatilla* helps the soft, gentle cat who has a bland yellow discharge, and *Kali bich.* if the discharge is yellow, tough and stringy. These remedies can be given in the *30C* potency twice daily. For chronic cases, *Silica 30C* can help where the infection has spread to the sinuses. If known, try the cat's constitutional remedy.

Where there may be a strong emotional component to the condition, caused by being in quarantine or in a cattery for example, you could try the Bach Flower *Heather* for loneliness, *Honeysuckle* for homesickness, and *Walnut* for difficulty in adapting to new circumstances.

Aromatherapy can also help to alleviate chronic symptoms, provided the cat can breathe fairly easily: *Eucalyptus*, *Pine* and *Thyme* can be used in a diffuser. Otherwise, try herbal infusions of *Garlic*, *Golden Seal* or *Liquorice*.

Tissue salts can also help to strengthen the cat in chronic cases: try *Kali mur.* if the discharge is white, *Kali sulph.* if it is yellow, or *Natrum mur.* if it is watery.

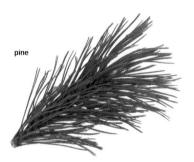

pine

garlic

△ ▽ The essential oils of both pine and garlic, burned in a vaporizer, can provide relief from some of the more chronic symptoms of cat flu.

foreign bodies

Grass awns stuck in a cat's nose may cause discharges. Cats have small noses, and it can be difficult to remove foreign bodies, even under anaesthetic. Consult your vet about suspected nasal obstructions. A rhinoscopy examination may be necessary as foreign bodies do not show up well on X-rays.

neoplasia

Nasal and sinus tumours may be a problem for older cats. Holistic therapies can be used to support conventional treatment.

▷ Catmint, or catnip, is used mainly as a feline stimulant, but a herbal infusion is helpful for catarrh.

Physical problems: the mouth and throat

Mouth problems in cats are common and can be caused by any number of reasons. Some problems can be prevented with due care, and most can be treated if caught in good time.

tooth care

The biggest problem seen in cats' mouths is neglected tartar, which can result in severe gum infections, and abscesses developing in gums and sinuses. The affected teeth will need descaling and possible extraction under anaesthetic. Use homeopathic *Merc. sol.*, before and after dentistry, to support the antibiotic prescribed by the vet.

A good natural tooth-cleaner is for your cat to chew on raw bones, as these seldom stick in its mouth. If your cat will not chew bones, then cleaning with special small brushes, or finger brushes is called for. Homeopathic *Frageria 6C*, given daily for several months, has a reputation for discouraging the development of tartar.

ulcers

Some cats develop ulcers on the lips and in the mouth which are not always associated with dental problems. The conventional

◁ Feeding raw bones to your cat will help to keep its teeth clean. Most cats are quite happy to source their own raw bones.

liquorice

thyme

◁ Infusions of liquorice can be given for coughs, while the essential oil of thyme can be massaged into sore throats.

antibiotics, steroids and female hormones are not very successful long-term. Homeopathic *Acid nit.*, given as a *30C* tablet twice daily for up to three weeks, can be more useful.

foreign bodies

Problems concerning objects stuck in the cat's mouth usually involve soft-cooked cartilage and bone sticking between the teeth. This results in excessive salivation and licking or chewing. Checks inside the cat's mouth while grooming can prevent this. Sewing needles are also a problem: the cat licks a piece of thread, and the spikes on its tongue mean that it has to swallow it. The needle is regurgitated, and impales itself on the back of the tongue. The needle can be removed under anaesthetic.

neoplasia

These may occur in the mouth and throat. Some are operable but if not, seek a referral to a holistic vet. Tumours are increasingly common in the thyroid gland of cats over 12 years old. The symptoms can look like renal failure – high thirst and weight loss in spite of a good appetite – but diagnosis is easy with a blood test. They can be treated by surgery coupled with holistic support.

◁ Cats need to be fit to catch their prey, and obesity will seriously affect hunting success.

holistic cat care

If your cat has a persistent cough, however mild, it should always be checked by the vet. It could be an indication of a more serious disease of either of the two major organs of the chest: the heart or the lungs.

If the cat has a persistent dry cough, which is brought on by exercise, it may be connected with its heart. If the heart is not working properly, body fluid can seep into the tissues causing swellings (oedema), and into the body cavities, causing dropsy. As the lungs fill with fluid, the cough gets worse, becoming soft and moist. Dropsy can also result from liver troubles; your vet will be able to tell you which organ is at fault.

If the cat's cough is connected with its heart, the vet will prescribe diuretics to remove excess fluid from the body and drugs that stimulate the heart and/or dilate the small blood vessels.

Complementary treatments can also work well and may reduce the amount of prescriptive drugs needed. The cough may have an emotional cause, with the cat

suffering some upset or distress before it started. In this case, try the Bach Flower remedies *Heather* for loneliness, *Star of Bethlehem* for emotional shock, and *Walnut* for difficulty in coping with changes.

A homeopathic vet may prescribe low-potency herbals or traditional herbals. Both of these can be very effective in well-chosen cases. A constitutional remedy may also be suggested to treat the underlying causes of the condition.

For home treatment, you can support conventional medication with homeo-pathic *Rumex crisp 6C* for dry coughs that are worse by day, and *Spongia 6C* for coughs that are worse at night. Give both remedies four times a day. If the pulse is very slow try *Digitalis 30C*, or *Carbo veg. 30C* when the slow pulse is accompanied by a desire for fresh, cool air. If the cat seems to have great pain in its chest, try *Cactus Grandiflora*. *Arsen. alb.* is often indicated if the cough causes restlessness around midnight, but *Lycopodium* is better for coughs that are worse between 4–8 a.m.

If the cat's limbs show signs of dropsical swelling, this can often be helped by *Apis mel.* The tissue salts *Calc fluor.*, given twice daily, can strengthen the heart muscles, and *Kali phos.* will help to stabilize abnormal heartbeats. Herbal infusions of *Dandelion* or *Hawthorn* may also help.

special diets

Cats with a heart condition should follow a low-salt diet. Special "heart diets" are available, containing less salt than normal foods; these are generally less appealing to choosy cats. Conventional diuretics can result in a loss of potassium from the body. To compensate, sprinkle seaweed powder (kelp), rich in vitamins and minerals, over food, or give the tissue salt *Kali phos.*

◁ Herbal infusions of mullein can soothe night-time coughs, whilst thyme, sage and liquorice are useful for most coughs.

△ The Bach Flower remedies can help illness caused by stress. Coughing in rehomed or kennelled cats responds to walnut, in particular.

lungs

Bronchitis is inflammation of the airways in the lungs. If this spreads to the actual lung tissue itself it can become pneumonia. The commonest cause is from cat flu, but deep wounds from fights or accidents, or wounds from air-gun pellets, can also develop into purulent pneumonia.

FIP is a viral infection in which the cavity surrounding the lungs fills with thick pus, whilst tumours of the chest may also occur in cats. X-rays and blood tests may be needed to identify these conditions as their symptoms are similar: both display a difficulty in breathing, with little coughing.

Antibiotics, coupled with steroids to control the inflammation, is the conven-tional treatment for chest infections. In the case of FIP it is often essential to drain pus from the cat's chest with a wide-bore needle to give the cat's lungs room to expand and reduce the workload of the antibiotics. In the short term, it may be necessary to use these drugs, but if long or repeated courses are prescribed, it may be worth considering holistic treatment.

For mild infections try aromatherapy inhalations of *Eucalyptus* if there is a lot of mucus on the chest, and *Tea-tree* or *Thyme* where pus is suspected.

If you prefer a homeopathic approach, *Aconite 6C* given frequently in the early stages of an infection is helpful, particularly

⊲ Many cats enjoy the snow, but chilling can affect their chests, lowering resistance and opening the way for infections to set in.

intervals, *Phosphorus* if there is blood in the sputum, *Kali carb.* if the cough is worse about 3 a.m., *Rumex crisp* if the cough is dry and worse by day, *Spongia* for a dry cough that is worse at night, and *Antimony tart* if there are rattling sounds in the chest.

Tissue salts can also help: try *Ferrum phos.* for harsh dry coughs, *Kali mur.* if the phlegm is white, and *Kali sulph.* when yellow phlegm is coughed up.

Herbal infusions of *Mullein* are good for night coughs, and *Thyme* and *Liquorice* are good for coughs in general. *Garlic* helps the immune system to combat infections but it may antidote some homeopathic remedies, so it is best avoided if the cat is having homeopathic treatment.

Asthma is becoming more common in cats. This is a chronic condition which is caused by a malfunction of the cat's immune system. A referral to a holistic vet would be beneficial. Homeopathic *Arsen. alb. 6C* or *Eucalyptus* essential oil may help in the interim.

aconite

where the cough is accompanied by a rise in temperature. *Belladonna* can be given if the cat becomes very fevered and its eyes dilate widely. Once the temperature begins to drop, try one of the following remedies, given four times a day: *Bryonia 6C* if the cat seems in pain when it moves, does not want to be touched and drinks a lot at long

⊲ Homeopathic aconite 6C can be given in the early stages of a cough, while the cat's temperature is still rising.

▽ Cats can be given medicine in food or water, provided that the cat can feed without getting the medicine on its nose.

Physical problems: the abdomen

Severe pain, vomiting and diarrhoea are likely to indicate a problem with one of the organs of the abdomen: the stomach, intestines, liver, pancreas, kidneys, bladder, or the sex organs (ovaries/uterus or prostate).

General abdominal pains will indicate intestinal or pancreatic troubles. Pain that is just behind the ribs is probably related to liver disease, and if it is in the triangle between the ribs and the back muscles, it probably relates to either the kidneys or the ovaries. If there is discomfort in the rear of the abdomen this may be a sign of bladder or prostate problems.

vomiting and/or diarrhoea

Physical symptoms such as vomiting and/or diarrhoea may result from either a primary or secondary inflammation of the stomach (gastritis), the small intestines (enteritis), or the large intestine (colitis). Primary gastritis and enteritis can be caused by food and other poisoning, eating too much rich food, foreign bodies or tumours. Foreign bodies in the stomach are actually very rare in cats – they usually eat too slowly and carefully to swallow anything that might block their intestines.

Worms are always present in kittens but sometimes these may become a problem. The small intestine becomes very active to rid the body of the worms and part of the bowel can get pushed out of place, which

causes a blockage that may need surgery. This involution is called an intussusception.

Pains in the stomach or intestines, as well as vomiting and diarrhoea may arise as a by-product of more serious diseases in the liver, kidney, or pancreas.

You should consult your vet if symptoms persist for more than 24 hours or if blood is present in the faeces. The vet will probably examine the cat for any foreign bodies or tumours and may take X-rays, especially if the vomiting is first thing in the morning. He or she may also take blood samples to see how the other organs are working, or take swabs for bacteriology tests.

Conventional treatment uses antibiotics to control infections, and steroids to dampen down the inflammation. Anabolics may be given for weight loss, insulin if the cat is diabetic, and intravenous fluids if the cat has lost a lot of fluid and is dehydrated. Dietary changes, vitamin and mineral supplements, and proprietary medical diets may also be suggested.

For complementary home treatment, an immediate first aid step is to stop feeding the cat. If there is vomiting, add a little salt to its drinking water and bicarbonate of soda if there is diarrhoea. If emotional factors could be involved, try the Bach Flowers: *Aspen* for fear, *Chicory* for separation anxiety, and *Impatiens* for the irritability associated with Irritable Bowel Syndrome.

△ **At the vet's surgery, careful palpatating of the abdomen of an ailing cat can reveal the organ that is most likely to be affected.**

Slippery Elm and *Arrowroot* soothe the intestines. These are available as powders which can be sprinkled on to the cat's food. Herbal infusions of *Gentian*, *St John's Wort* and *Peppermint* will also ease the stomach.

Homeopathic *Arsen. alb.* is probably the first remedy to think of for vomiting and diarrhoea, particularly if it's been brought on by food poisoning. Symptoms are worse around midnight, the cat is restless and will sip a little water at frequent intervals. *Phosphorus* can be tried for thirsty cats who drink a lot but then regurgitate it after 15–20 minutes. If the vomiting starts after too much rich food, *Nux vom.* is useful. *Ipecacuana* is for persistent vomiting and diarrhoea that comes on after eating indigestible foods, when there is often blood and mucus in the faeces. Try *Aloes* for diarrhoea with flatulence and *Podophyllum* if the stools are watery. *Chamomilla* helps teething kittens, especially if the stools

▷ **The amount and manner in which a cat drinks can be an important guide to the appropriate homeopathic remedy.**

peppermint

△ Peppermint is a great bowel tonic. It reduces both gas and vomiting and eases chronic colitis.

△ Not all cats dislike water. However, if the temperature of the water is too cold it can bring on cystitis. When your cat is outside, you will have very little control over its movements.

are a greenish colour, and *Capiscum* helps rehomed kittens suffering from recurrent bouts of pale-coloured diarrhoea. In all cases the *6C* potency can be used at short intervals, lengthening the time between doses as the condition improves.

Tissue salts can also be tried: *Ferrum phos.* if the cat is bringing back undigested food, *Kali mur.* if the vomit is thick mucus, *Natrum phos.* if it is sour and acidic, and *Natrum sulph.* for yellow green bile. Give *Kali phos.* for diarrhoea due to anxiety, or *Natrum mur.* if diarrhoea alternates with constipation. As the cat shows signs of recovery, start feeding it with small bland meals of cooked fish or chicken (off the bone), together with rice or pasta.

△ Homeopathic capiscum (red pepper) will resolve the diarrhoea of newly-rehomed kittens.

liver and kidneys

If your cat has lost its appetite, is bringing up bile and has pain around its ribs it may have problems with its liver. Jaundice is also caused by liver disease. Kidney trouble can show either as an absence of thirst or else a great thirst with vomiting. If the trouble is chronic it can lead to loss of appetite, high thirst and vomiting, increased urination, weight loss and dehydration. All of these symptoms need referring to a vet.

The Bach Flower *Crab Apple* will help to detoxify the body and should be given in the first instance for problems with the liver and kidneys. Herbal infusions of *Barberry* are also good for both organs, whilst infusions of *Dandelion* are good for the liver and *Bearberry* for the kidneys. Try aromatherapy inhalations of *Rosemary* for the liver, and *Juniper* for the kidneys and bladder.

In homeopathic terms, give *Lycopodium* for liver problems which are worse around 4 p.m. If jaundice is caught in its early stages, and where there is vomiting, give *Chelidonium*. Try *Carduus marianus* for dropsy and jaundice if there are hard dry stools. Kidney problems with intense thirst, weight loss and greasy fur usually respond to *Natrum mur*. *Merc. sol*. helps if the cat has excessive saliva and ulcers begin to form in its mouth, and *Kali chlor.* helps if its breath is putrid and the ulcers are a greyish colour.

pancreas

Both inflammation of the pancreas and diabetes need veterinary diagnosis and treatment. Homeopathic *Iris ver.* can be tried but constitutional treatment from an expert is really needed.

bladder

Veterinary tests are needed to differentiate between infections, gallstones and simple incontinence. Complementary therapies are very useful once the cause is known. Homeopathic *Cantharis 6C* or *Merc. sol. 6C*, given every hour, can help if there is a sudden onset of straining to pass blood-stained urine. If stones are present, try *Berberis 6C*, and *Thalaspi Bursa 6C* if there are lots of crystals. Incontinence of old age often responds well to *Caustisum*.

▷ Inhalations of rosemary aid liver troubles and juniper those of the kidneys and bladder. Do make sure the diffuser is safe from being knocked over.

Physical problems: the skin

The skin is the biggest organ of a cat's body. It forms a barrier against the outside world, protects the body against the elements and helps to control the body temperature. Sweat and sebum are waste matter produced in the sebaceous glands of the body which are excreted via the skin. The skin is usually the first place where signs of any inner disease are detected.

In disease, the body's metabolism becomes disturbed and the secretions from the sebaceous glands are changed. This is followed by changes in the skin's micro-climate that allow the development of infections and other skin diseases.

Orthodox skin treatments are excellent at reducing the pain and inflammation that accompanies acute skin conditions, but, unfortunately, they rarely correct the underlying imbalance. In fact, prolonged or repeated skin treatment can suppress symptoms, which can lead to chronic, and sometimes drug-induced, disease.

Chronic skin conditions are based upon malnutrition, hormonal imbalances, and emotional problems that stress the immune system and open the way for bacterial or fungal infections, parasitic infestations and allergies. All chronic skin conditions can be helped by complementary treatment.

parasites

The main external parasites of cats are fleas, lice, harvest mites, ticks and burrowing mites. Fleas are small reddish-brown insects that move and jump through the fur. Lice are small, slow-moving grey insects, normally found on the ear flaps. Tiny red or orange harvest mites can be found on the ears and between the toes in late summer and autumn. Ticks bite the skin and then suck the cat's blood for several days; burrowing mites are found on the cat's head.

Almost every cat owner will know the nuisance caused by one or other of these parasites. Apart from the fact that they are unpleasant and annoying for both cat and owner, the main signifi-cance is that some parasites can transmit disease to humans. Fleas can spread the bubonic plague in areas where the disease still exists in wildlife, and ticks commonly spread blood parasites, the cause of tick-borne fevers in humans.

Conventional treatments involve the use of chemicals to kill the insects, both on and off the animal. Always follow the instructions with care as overuse can cause problems.

◁ The cat's coat should be sleek. The first signs of stress or chronic disease will often appear in the skin and the coat.

lavender

◁ The essential oil of lavender can be used as an insect repellent if well diluted with water. It also has a sedative effect.

Complementary treatments aim to repel the insects rather than kill them. Plastic hooks are available from your vet that will safely remove ticks. *Xenex* is a herbal product that has been demonstrated to repel fleas for up to 40 days. Herbal *Garlic* given daily and homeopathic *Sulphur 30C* used weekly are also reputed to repel insects; use one or the other but not both. Three drops of one of the essential oils of *Cedarwood, Eucalyptus, Lavender, Lemon, Mint, Rosemary* or *Terebinth* added to 150 ml (¼ pint) of water can be brushed into the coat, although the cat probably won't like the smell on its fur.

Ringworm is hard to detect in cats. There may be no outward signs at all, as it does not cause the red round itchy spots and rings in cats that it does in dogs. Sometimes the cat may have a little mild dandruff and some cats get a very scurfy

coat. Cats can pass ringworm on to humans. The treatment is applications of conventional lotion supported by homeopathic *Baccillinum 200* weekly or *Tellurium 30C* weekly. Again, the essential oils of *Lavender* or *Tea-tree* can be tried.

Complementary support for all skin troubles can be given. Try homeopathic *Sulphur* for cats that dislike the warmth, or *Psorinum* for those that hate the cold. Herbal *Garlic* tablets have a beneficial effect on the skin but can antidote homeopathic remedies. The tissue salt *Calc. sulph.* is usually good for skin disorders, and the essential oils of *Lavender*, *Lemon* and *Wild Marjoram* can be used in a diluted form in the same way as for skin parasites above.

allergies

Skin allergies and eczema are usually skin manifestations of an internal disorder, often with an emotional basis. The removal of the allergy provoking trigger (if known) will obviously keep the cat's symptoms at bay, but if it comes into contact with the substance again in the future, the allergic reaction will most likely recur.

A good holistic treatment could cure the underlying problem. If you can't get a referral to a suitable practitioner, some home treatments can be tried. If emotional factors are involved, try the Bach Flowers *Agrimony* where there is underlying anxiety; *Crab Apple* if the cat is toxic with matted fur and secondary skin infections; and *Holly* to help allergies in the more malicious cat.

◁ A compress made from an infusion of oak bark can help to relieve hot, red skin lesions.

Aromatherapy with *Rosemary* and *Lavender*, or *Lavender*, *Pine* and *Terebinth* does help, but the oils should be diluted and kept away from the affected areas of skin. Burning the same oils in a diffuser in the room where the cat has its basket can also help. The indications for homeopathic *Sulphur* and *Psorinum* have been discussed above, but homeopathic *Apis mel.* is useful for allergies where the skin is shiny, red and better for cold applications, and *Urtica urens* if the skin is better for warmth. *Natrum mur.* can be indicated when there is a possibility of long-standing grief: the skin looks greasy and the fur seems clumped together like a paintbrush. Herbal infusions of *Oak Bark* or decoctions of *Mallow* can be applied as compresses to soothe hot, red skin; *Aloe vera* gel can also help to soothe and calm inflammation. Nutritional support with *Evening Primrose Oil* and fish oils also helps; continue this even when the skin improves.

Physical problems: the female system

Because of the modern-day tendency to neuter female cats, problems of the female reproductive tract are far less common now than in the past. Today, ovarian infections are rare, although ovarian cysts can occur and lead to infertility or abortions. These are difficult to treat by any system, orthodox or complementary.

The Bach Flower remedy *Scleranthus* can help to restore balance to a disturbed system and may help if the cat has a history of regular abortions. Herbal infusions of *Raspberry Leaf* can also be tried. Ideally, a homeopathic consultation would help. *Sepia* and *Pulsatilla* are the remedies most concerned with female hormone balance, but there are others. *Viburnum 30C* given weekly during the first three weeks after mating, and *Caulophyllum 30C* given weekly during the last three weeks, have helped some queens who have problems with miscarriage.

Metritis is when the uterus becomes inflamed, usually from infections that arise during abortions or after giving birth. If neglected, the condition can worsen and the uterus fill with pus (pyometritis). Pyometritis may also result from a hormonal imbalance. The uterus becomes cystic and then fills with the cysts' contents as they rupture.

The result of both metritis and pyometritis is an unhappy cat with a messy vaginal discharge. In rare cases, the cervix remains closed and the cat's belly swells as the pus builds up inside. She may develop a high temperature and a high thirst. If the condition develops rapidly, surgery may be necessary to remove the ovaries and uterus. If the condition is in the early stages, complementary treatment may stop the disease and prevent the need for surgery.

The Bach Flower remedy *Scleranthus* can be tried to restore normal hormone balance. Homeopathic remedies can be given in the *30C* potency, up to four times a day. The choice of remedy is based mainly on the type of discharge: *Sepia* for brownish discharges, *Caulophyllum* for chocolate brown ones, *Pulsatilla* for bland creamy yellow ones, *Hydrastis* for a white mucoid one and *Sabina* if fresh blood is present. Herbal infusions of *Golden Seal* and *Myrrh* may help, and the tissue salt *Calc sulph.* can also be given.

△ A herbal infusion of myrrh has both antiseptic and anti-inflammatory properties. It can help in cases of abnormal discharges.

▷ Homeopathic sepia and pulsatilla are the most commonly needed remedies for female problems. Infusions of golden seal also help.

△ It can be difficult to tell a diseased uterus from a healthy one by feel alone, even for experts at the vet's surgery.

△ Further investigations, such as blood tests and X-rays, may be needed if the cervix is closed and there are no discharges.

Physical problems: the male tract

The male tract of the cat comprises the testicles and penis. Cats do not have a prostate gland. Since the vast majority of tom cats are castrated before they are six months old, medical conditions of the male reproductive tract are relatively rare.

The most common cause of problems in the testes is through injuries gained while fighting. This area is the prime target during cat fights, followed by the eyes and ears. This accounts for the large number of bite wounds typically seen around the base of a tom's tail and on its head.

The result of cat bites is usually an infection causing pain and swelling. These bites should always be seen by a vet, and the treatment should be supported by homeopathic remedies. In the first stage, when the cat is running a high temperature, *Belladonna 30C* can be given every hour for four doses. The cat's pupils will be dilated and the area around the testes will be red, hot and painful. If pus is present or

◁ The Bach Flower remedy scleranthus can often help to stabilize the behaviour of over-sexed tom cats.

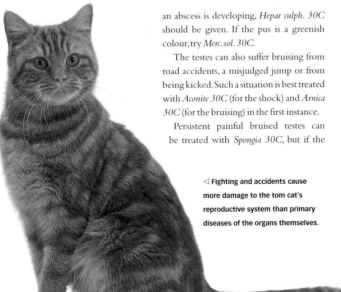

◁ Fighting and accidents cause more damage to the tom cat's reproductive system than primary diseases of the organs themselves.

an abscess is developing, *Hepar sulph. 30C* should be given. If the pus is a greenish colour, try *Merc. sol. 30C*.

The testes can also suffer bruising from road accidents, a misjudged jump or from being kicked. Such a situation is best treated with *Aconite 30C* (for the shock) and *Arnica 30C* (for the bruising) in the first instance.

Persistent painful bruised testes can be treated with *Spongia 30C*, but if the

testes are swollen and harder than normal, *Clematis* may be better. The Bach Flower *Rescue Remedy* should be given for all testicular trauma and the tissue salt *Ferrum phos.* can also help.

If the scrotum is ruptured in an accident, leaving the testes exposed and hanging free, surgical removal is the best option. Only if the tom is a valuable stud cat would it be worth having the damage repaired.

Some toms may develop hyper-sexual behaviour due to an overproduction of male hormones. Unless the cat is wanted for stud purposes, castration is strongly recommended. Alternatively, the Bach Flower remedy *Scleranthus* may bring hormonal production under control, and homeopathic *Ustilago maydis* or *Pulsatilla* may help to a certain degree to subdue the cat. Holistic treatments for aggressive behaviour may also be useful before serious fighting breaks out.

Physical problems: the hormone system

Hormone production plays an important role in keeping the body working healthily and efficiently. Hormones are produced by the endocrine glands and are then secreted into the bloodstream and carried round to the body's tissues and organs.

The pituitary, adrenal and ovaries are three glands which together control the female reproductive system. The body's metabolic rate is controlled by the thyroid gland, while the pancreas controls glucose metabolism as well as producing digestive enzymes. The adrenal gland, in addition to its reproductive role, produces many steroids (including cortisone) and these control many functions.

Cushing's disease is when the body is producing too much cortisone. This may be due to tumours of the pituitary gland or of the adrenal itself. Addison's disease is an under-production of cortisone. This can result from the adrenal gland's capacity being suppressed by overuse of steroid drugs, or by tumours of the adrenal gland.

◁ Homeopathic sarcodes can help to restore the function of diseased endocrine glands. These are not available as over-the-counter products, and should only be used under the supervision of a vet.

iris

▷ Homeopathic iris ver. 30C plus aloe vera gel can help reduce the need for insulin in cats with diabetes.

Both these diseases and diabetes can lead to weakness, lethargy and great thirst in the cat. Loss of fur may be seen in Cushing's disease and in under-activity of the thyroid (hypothyroidism).

An overactive thyroid gland (hyperthyroidism) is characterized by a high thirst, weight loss, a rapid heartbeat and marked hyperactivity and irritability.

If any hormonal imbalance is suspected in your cat, you should see a vet who will carry out blood tests to find out exactly what is wrong. Hormonal deficiencies are best treated by replacement therapy, using insulin for diabetes and thyroid extract for hypothyroidism. An overactive thyroid is best treated by surgery.

Holistic support can improve the quality of the cat's life and reduce the amount of conventional treatment needed. Therefore, you should let the vet know if you are giving remedies and the cat's blood hormone levels should be monitored regularly to check their effect.

The Bach Flower *Scleranthus* can support any endocrine gland, as does the tissue salt *Natrum mur.* Homeopathic preparations of

normal healthy glands (sarcodes) can help if given as a *30C* potency every week: *Pancreatinum* for the pancreas, *Thyroidinum* for the thyroid, *Cortisone* for the adrenals and *Pituitin* for the pituitary. In addition, *Iodum* or *Natrum mur.* may benefit hyperthyroidism, and *Iris ver.* the pancreas. Use both remedies in the *30C* potency, weekly. *Syzygium 6C* helps to stabilize insulin production and *Thyroidinum 6X* can help as a replacement for thyroid extract. Herbal tablets of *Seaweed* and *Garlic* are used for hypothyroidism, and *Dandelion*, *Nettle* and *Parsley* infusions have been used for adrenal problems.

▽ Herbal infusions of parsley have a diuretic effect that can help to control the dropsy seen in both Cushing's and Addison's disease.

parsley

A network of nerves runs throughout the cat's whole body. These nerves carry instructions to and from the brain, and they branch off from the spinal cord. It is the brain, nerves, and spinal cord which make up the nervous system.

Convulsions in cats are usually due to poisoning, particularly from slug-bait or anti-freeze. They can also be caused by epilepsy, diabetes, physical injuries, brain tumours and chronic infections. A cat may begin to shake, go rigid, lose its balance, fall over and have violent muscle spasms when it is having a convulsion. Although these may be violent, they are not painful. The cat should be left in a cool, dark, quiet place to recover, and taken to the vet when the convulsions stop. If, however, the convulsions continue for more than ten minutes, or if they recur, then the cat should be put in a padded box and taken to the vet as an emergency.

Other effects of inflammation of the brain and its membranes are behavioural changes, pain, loss of balance and limb

▽ The Bach Flower remedy cherry plum is often used following epileptiform convulsions, usually in conjunction with aspen.

paralysis. These can result from infections – including a feline form of mad cow/variant CJD disease – and tumours. Uncontrollable twitching (chorea) can also result from brain disease.

All these conditions will need urgent investigation by a vet, who may prescribe anti-convulsants and antibiotics. Holistic care can be used in support.

The Bach Flower *Rescue Remedy* can be given at the onset of symptoms and this can

be followed by *Cherry Plum* to restore control of "crazy" behaviour in the cat. Aromatherapy, using diffusions of *Lavender* and *Chamomile* oils, can help. The homeo-pathic remedy *Belladonna* is good for fitting cats with dilated eyes, and *Stramonium* helps those who fall to the left. Both can be given in the *30C* potency every fifteen minutes to begin with. *Cocculus 30C*, given weekly, has been used as a long-term preventative of fits, while *Cuprum met.* or *Zincum met.* will help to control chorea if given daily as *6C*. Herbal infusions of *Skullcap* and *Valerian* may also help as they have a sedative effect.

Neuralgia is a painful condition when the nerves themselves become inflamed. It can cause self-trauma from scratching or biting at the affected area. Nerve pain, following heavy blows and crushing injuries, will respond well to homeopathic *Hypericum*, teething pains to *Chamomilla*, and other neuralgias to *Colocynth* if the pains are on the left side or *Mag. phos.* if they are on the right. The tissue salt *Mag. phos.* can be used for all neuralgias. *Lavender* oil, diluted in a carrier oil, may be massaged into the area if the skin is undamaged, and herbal infusions of *Passiflora* may help.

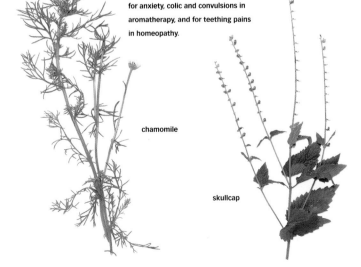

◁ Chamomile is used as a herbal infusion for anxiety, colic and convulsions in aromatherapy, and for teething pains in homeopathy.

chamomile

skullcap

◁ Skullcap is used mainly with valerian, in the form of herbal infusions or tablets, as a sedative.

Physical problems: the locomotor system

Cats are renowned for their agility and dexterity. Most of us have probably been impressed to see a cat jump from a high spot and land lightly on its feet, or have held our breath as we watch it pick its way across a narrow shelf, nonchalantly stepping over precious china.

The strength and mobility of the cat are dependent on the healthy functioning of the locomotor system – the joints, muscles and bones of its body. Malfunction of any of these parts is usually accompanied by pain, which may be acute or chronic. The onset of severe, sudden pain is usually the result of accidents or acute infections, whilst a more continuous, low-grade pain is the sign of a chronic condition.

acute conditions

Cats falling from heights above 5 m (15 ft) will land on their feet but not always safely. They can suffer compression fractures of their limbs, and may suffer injuries of their mouth, chest and abdomen as their legs unfold. The number and severity of the injuries will get worse with heights up to 15 m (45 ft); above this height the injuries will be on a similar level of seriousness.

If your cat is involved in an accident and is in great pain, is showing signs of lameness, or is unconscious, then it should be seen by

◁ **Cats seldom fall, and when they do they land on their feet. The impact, however, can be too great for their limbs to withstand.**

a vet as soon as possible. Low-grade pain and stiffness that lasts for more than five days should also be checked at the veterinary surgery, so that any necessary X-rays can be taken.

All fractures and dislocations will need surgical treatment. The conventional treatment for pain relief is either by a course of non-steroidal, anti-inflammatory drugs or by steroids. Cats, in general, do not respond well to non-steroidal drugs, and aspirin is particularly toxic to them – the dosage recommendation is one-hundredth of that for an adult human.

Acute infections may also bring on pain which is sudden and severe. Cat bites should always be taken seriously. Typically, the wounds are deep and penetrating and can cause painful infections of both the muscles (myositis) and the bones (osteitis). Acute infections will usually need treatment by antibiotics, and these should be prescribed by the vet.

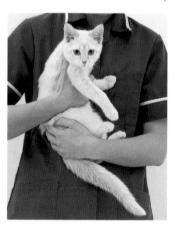

◁ **It is not always obvious that a cat has suffered internal injuries in an accident. The cat should be checked over by a vet.**

The Bach Flower *Rescue Remedy* or *Aconite 30C* should be given for shock as soon as possible after any accident. This can be followed by *Arnica 30C* to help with bruising and for pain relief. If the vet has confirmed that there are no fractures and dislocations, then acupuncture, osteopathy or chiropractic can be tried. These may be supported by physiotherapy, TTouch or simple massage. Reiki can also be helpful. If the skin is unbroken, you can try essential oil of *Rosemary* in a cat massage.

Although homeopathic *Arnica* is the standard remedy for bruising, *Bryonia* may also be indicated when the cat refuses to use its injured limb. Both of these can be followed by *Ruta grav.* and *Rhus tox.* as the cat improves. Use *6C* up to four times a day.

Antibiotic treatment can be supported with *Hepar sulph. 30C* for muscles and joint infections, but a higher potency, such as a *200C*, may be better if the bones are involved. If it does not help you can try *Calc. Fluor. 6C* until the pus finds a way to the surface. All bone and joint surgery should be supported with *Arnica 30C*, at the time of the operation, and *Arnica* or *Bryonia*

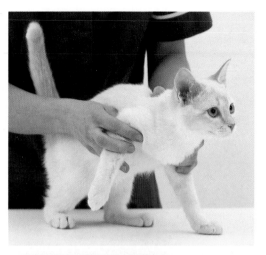

◁ Gentle manipulation of the limbs will usually indicate the existence of any fractures or dislocations. Comparing the limbs on both sides of the cat's body will show its original range of movement.

▽ Simple, manipulative physiotherapy by a trained therapist has its place in treatment if there is no bone damage present.

arnica

△ Herbal creams and ointments are available for external use on bruises. Homeopathic preparations can be taken by mouth for internal damage.

fixed routine. Homeopathic *Rhus tox.* is useful for restless cats suffering from the classical rheumatic stiffness that is worse in cold damp weather and better for gentle exercise; *Causticum* helps those who are prematurely stiff, particularly if they are prone to cystitis; *Caulophyllum* will help when the small joints, such as the knee and hock, are involved. Use these remedies as a *6C* daily. *Calc. fluor. 30C* given weekly, can help to dissolve boney changes.

Dietary supplements of *Evening Primrose Oil*, royal jelly and a weekly dose of 300mg of cod liver oil can all help to maintain joint flexibility. Glucosamine, chondroitin sulphate and green-lipped mussel extract are all useful for arthritis in humans; cats need about half the dosage, but check these with your vet before feeding to your cat. Magnetic collars also seem to be helpful for cats suffering from pains in the joints.

afterwards, depending on the cat's attitude to movement. Further support can be given with weekly doses of *Calc. phos.*, to balance calcium metabolism, and *Symphytum*, to stimulate the activity of the cells that repair the bones.

chronic conditions

Rheumatism and arthritis are chronic conditions which cause low-grade pain in either the muscles (rheumatism) or joints (arthritis). In general, cats are not as prone to these diseases as larger animals, as their relatively small size puts less strain on their limbs. These diseases are sometimes seen, however, in older cats.

Under the guidance of the vet, acupuncture, physiotherapy and the various massage therapies can help a cat suffering from rheumatic pains. The Bach Flowers can also help. *Beech* is indicated for cats that are rigid and stiff with pain; *Impatiens* for those that are tetchy and irritable; and *Rock Water* can help to restore physical flexibility to cats that have become mentally rigid and need a

Bone tumours can occur in cats and they are always painful. These tumours are not as aggressive in cats as they are in dogs and other animals, and surgery is very often successful if the tumour appears on one of the limbs. While conventional treatment is advised for tumours, holistic care can be used in a supporting role (see *Neoplasia*).

brewer's yeast

evening primrose

◁ Brewer's yeast and evening primrose oil can benefit cats as much as humans.

Physical problems: neoplasia

For reasons we don't yet fully understand, the cells of the body can begin to multiply uncontrollably, forming new growths (neoplasia). These growths are commonly referred to under the umbrella heading of cancer, although, strictly speaking, the term tumour is used for benign neoplasms, whilst cancer applies to neoplasms which are malignant.

causes of neoplasia

Benign tumours are considered non-life-threatening: they do not spread to other parts of the body and usually have a clearly defined edge. Because of this, they are relatively easy to remove in surgery. Sometimes, however, they are difficult to remove and can become life-threatening, either because of their size or because of the impact they have on other organs. For example, a small brain tumour can cause problems because of its location.

Malignant growths, on the other hand, are not so clearly defined. These growths send tentacles of abnormal cells into the adjacent tissues and it becomes impossible to tell the difference between what is healthy and what is abnormal. The growths can also spread around the body through the blood or lymphatic system. These two factors make surgery less successful.

Neoplasms range from harmless warts (papillomas) at one end of the scale to highly malignant cancers that can kill a cat in a few weeks. Current medical science recognizes that neoplasms can develop after exposure to cancer-inducing agents, known as carcinogens. Inhaling tobacco smoke, the effect of sunlight and radioactive materials, some chemicals and certain infections, for example, are known to increase the risk of cancer in humans, and the same factors also seem to apply to cats.

There is a tendency for some cats to develop cancer of the ear. This is caused by overexposure to bright sunlight on the often pale and delicate skin in this area. Cats are also susceptible to specific viral infections that can cause cancers. The two most important are Feline Leukaemia (FeLV) and the Feline Immunodeficiency Virus (FIV). Both of these diseases are, at present, incurable.

Although cats can be vaccinated against FeLV, as yet there is no vaccine against FIV. FIV affects the cat in a similar way to the human AIDS virus; it is not transmissible to humans. Both of these diseases cause a wide range of symptoms, often including swollen lymph glands. Cats with strange symptoms, especially with gland enlargement, should be tested by the vet as soon as possible.

treatment options

Conventional knife surgery, laser surgery, chemotherapy and radiotherapy are all used in the treatment of malignant tumours. The holistic viewpoint sees the cancer as the body's attempt to store potentially toxic material – produced as a result of a reaction to carcinogens – which it is unable to

△ Holistic treatment of cats with cancer reduces the side effects of conventional therapy and improves the quality of the patient's life.

excrete. Malignant neoplasms represent the end point of a disease process that may have been going on for weeks, months or years.

We do not know exactly why neoplasms occur in the first place, but it seems certain that they are likely to grow when early and apparently minor symptoms are ignored, or when the animal's vitality is weak and it is unable to respond to therapy. Sometimes treatment is unsuccessful and the cancer continues to grow, or else returns soon after an apparent reprieve.

The body's attempts to cope with cancer are affected by physical and mental stress factors. Good complementary therapy will help to strengthen the animal's immune system, and may even halt or reverse the disease process. Several veterinary practices have reported a decrease in the number of cancer cases they see after having introduced holistic methods into the practice. They have also noticed long-lasting remissions following complementary treatment in cases that would, otherwise, have almost certainly been terminal.

◁ Herbal infusions can be of help. Red clover has an effect on cancers in general, and autumn crocus relieves their pains.

▷ The same vegetables that have been found to help humans will also help cats. They can be liquidized and poured over the cat's normal diet to provide anti-cancer nutrition in the form of antioxidants and essential vitamins.

aloe vera

broccoli

royal jelly supplement

garlic

beetroot (beets)

carrots

If your cat has cancer, deciding which therapies to try is a personal choice and all options should be discussed with the vet. The best approach is usually a combination of conventional and complementary methods. If the cat is too weak to undergo orthodox treatment, such as radiotherapy, complementary treatment may help to build up the cat's vitality to facilitate its use later on. Surgery should always be supported by complementary remedies to help with the trauma, while the side effects of chemotherapy or radiotherapy can be reduced with complementary remedies. Once the active treatment is over, an holistic attempt can be made to treat the underlying cause of the disease.

It is difficult to assess the outcome of the various treatments for cancer objectively. Most people would consider the disappearance of the neoplasm a success, particularly if it doesn't return over a reasonably long time period. This result may be obtained by both conventional and complementary treatment. Many owners would consider the treatment successful if it helps their pet to have a calm, relatively pain-free, natural death, as opposed to the end of its life being one of suffering. Holistic treatment is certainly beneficial in this respect.

holistic care

The Bach Flowers *Agrimony, Gentian, Gorse, Impatiens, Mustard, Oak,* and *Olive* have all been found to help in cancer cases, the selection being based on the cat's mental state at the time. Reiki, TTouch, various massage techniques and acupuncture have been used to bring calm and balance to the cat, and to relieve pain.

Homeopathy is useful to support and reduce the side effects of conventional medicine and will treat the underlying cause of the cancer. *Arnica* helps to reduce bruising and pain and both *Hypericum* and *Calendula* can help the skin to heal after surgery. *Calc phos.* and *Symphytum* are useful

if bone tissue is affected. *Uranium 30C* is useful for the side effects of radiotherapy as it helps with radiation sickness. Non-specific support can be given by *Viscum album, Echinacea,* which strengthens the immune system generally, and *Hydrastis* or *Eupatorium perfoliatum,* which both help to relieve pains. *Arsen. alb.,* given in rising potencies, can remove the fear of dying from a terminally ill cat, and will allow a peaceful transition from life to death.

The tissue salt *Calc. phos.* is useful for stimulating the body's metabolism, whilst *Echinacea* may be given to the cat as a herbal infusion, rather than homeopathically, if preferred. Other herbal infusions which are helpful are *Red Clover,* as an all-purpose anti-cancer treatment, and *Autumn Crocus* for pain relief. The infusions should be given twice daily.

Anthroposophical preparations of herbal mistletoe (*Viscum abnova* and *Iscador*) are used successfully for human sufferers. This is expensive and not widely used at present, but it is a valid therapy, and it should form part of the discussion with your vet.

Dietary changes will also help. Adding antioxidant-rich vegetables, plus vitamin supplements, royal jelly and garlic to the diet can benefit cats as much as humans.

Holistic medicine may not cure cancer, but it will help to reduce the suffering, and can extend the period of quality life for you and your cat.

▽ The Bach Flower remedies are useful in treating cancers. Base your choice of remedies on the cat's emotional state.

First aid treatments

Many complementary therapies are suitable for first aid in the home and it is probably worth investing in a few to create your own natural remedy first aid kit. However, although it is valid for a cat's owner to give their pet first aid for minor conditions, any animal involved in a serious accident must always be checked by a vet.

artificial respiration

In an emergency situation where your cat is injured and not moving it is worth trying artificial respiration while you wait for the vet. Begin by checking to see if the cat is conscious by pinching the web between its toes. If the cat is awake it will quickly pull its paw back. If it doesn't, look to see if its chest is moving. Movement in the chest shows that the cat is breathing. If there are no signs of movement, make sure that nothing is stuck in its throat and/or nose – blood, mucus or foreign bodies can get stuck in these places. If the airways are clear

and the cat still does not breathe, close its mouth with one hand and very gently blow down its nose. Its chest should rise as air enters its lungs. Keep the lungs inflated for a count of three, then let the air out naturally. Repeat this at 5-10 second intervals.

Between puffs, feel for the heartbeat by touching the ribcage. If there is no heartbeat, cardiac massage can be given by squeezing the chest between the fingers and thumb of one hand once or twice every second. Alternate the blowing and squeezing every 15-20 seconds. If the heartbeat restarts, artificial respiration can be kept up for 20 minutes. If the heartbeat does not restart within four minutes, the cat has died.

bleeding

If your cat is bleeding heavily try to put a layer of wadding (batting) material over the wound and bandage it firmly. Many cats may resist this, in which case wrap the cat in a blanket or towel, put it in a suitable

carrier and get it to the vet as quickly as you can. If possible, let the vet know you are coming. The first aid treatment for the shock that accompanies any accident is two drops of the Bach Flower *Rescue Remedy* or homeopathic *Aconite 6C* or *30C*. These medicines can also be given to unconscious cats because they will be absorbed through the lining of the mouth.

wounds

Serious wounds must always receive professional help. Cuts and bruises can result from many causes, such as traffic accidents and cat fights. If necessary, treat the cat for shock and bleeding, as above. This can be followed by homeopathic *Arnica 30C*, the ideal first medicine for all cuts and bruises. If the bruising is severe, a change to *Bellis perennis* may be needed after a couple of days. *Hypericum 12C* helps all crushing injuries of the legs and tail, and *Calendula 6C* helps minor cuts and grazes to heal. If blood

treating wounds Fight wounds and road accidents are always accompanied by a degree of shock. Always give either Rescue Remedy or aconite before doing anything else. Minor wounds can be cleaned and dressed before seeing a vet. If there is a lot of bleeding, use thick padding and bandage as firmly as the cat will allow.

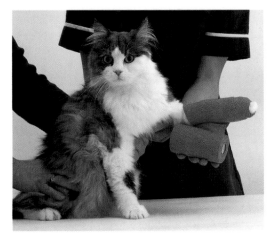

△ **1** Having removed any objects from the wound and after cleaning it, apply a bandage to cover it, using a non-stick dressing and a soft cotton bandage. It may need two people: one to comfort the cat, the other to treat it.

△ **2** In an emergency, masking tape or adhesive tape may be used instead of elastoplast to hold the dressing in place. Take the adhesive bandage 2.5 cm (1 in) up the fur to prevent it from slipping off.

spurts from the wound, *Phosphorus 30C* will help, if it flows more smoothly from the wound use *Ipecacuana*, and if there is dark-coloured blood use *Hamamelis 12C*. A tablet of the tissue salt *Ferrum phos.* can be crushed and sprinkled on to bleeding wounds. Minor wounds can be cleaned with *Hypercal* tincture diluted 1:10, and *Hypercal* cream can be used as a dressing. Essential oils of *Lavender* or *Terebinth* may be massaged around the injury, but do not use them directly on the injured part.

burns and scalds

A burn is caused by dry heat and scalds by moist heat or steam. The kitchen is usually where these kinds of injuries occur. The cat's curiosity may lead it to jump on to a still-hot ring on the hob, for example.

Do not put grease on burns but bathe them with cold water. If fat has been spilt on the fur it may be necessary to trim some of it away. *Rescue Remedy* or homeopathic *Aconite* should be given as for shock. If there is blistering, *Cantharis* will help, while the essential oils of *Lavender* and *Rosemary* may be massaged around, but not on, the area.

◁ The Bach Flower Rescue Remedy will help to calm an injured cat and make it easier to administer first aid.

◁ Clean any oils or creosote from the fur as quickly as possible. They are absorbed through the cat's highly-absorbent skin and can poison its liver.

bites and stings

Cat fights are common and the bites received frequently turn septic. *Rescue Remedy* and *Aconite* can be given for shock. This should be followed by *Ledum 30C* for penetrating wounds that are more painful than they look. One or two doses at ten minute intervals can be given. If the bites develop into painful abscesses, give homeopathic *Hepar sulph. 30C* every two hours. Chronic non-painful ones should be treated with *Silica 30C* daily until they heal. Herbal tablets of *Garlic* or *Echinacea* will aid the healing. Dog bites tear the skin and muscles, and should be treated in the same way as any other wound.

Insect bites and stings are very common because of the cat's habit of chasing after bees and wasps. These wounds are best treated with *Apis mel. 30C* every 15 minutes if they appear swollen, red and better for cold bathing, while *Urtica urens* works well on those that are better for warmth.

poisoning

If you suspect poisoning, contact the vet immediately. It is unusual for a cat to swallow human tablets, but if you think it has, let the vet know the name and quantity. Poisoning by slug-bait is common. Do not try to make the cat vomit, unless advised to do so by the vet. *Rescue Remedy*, followed by *Crab Apple*, will detoxify the cat. Homeopathic *Nux vom. 30C* is also a good detoxifier. *Veratrum alb. 30C* can be given every 15 minutes if the cat is cold, collapsed and has diarrhoea. If oil has been spilt on its fur, the fur should be cut away or washed, if the cat will allow it.

The death of your cat

Like the seasons, the cycle of birth, life and death follows a natural and unbreakable cycle that will always be completed. It is a widely held view that the essential life source of any living being, human or animal, continues to exist beyond physical death, perhaps rejoining the one invisible, universal source of all living things.

Whatever is the case, eventually the responsibility will fall upon you to see that your cat has as peaceful a transition from life to death as possible. The most desirable scenario is that when death approaches, your cat will die quietly in its sleep, or that you will be on hand to comfort it. Often, however, dying is a slow and painful process and you may be forced to make the difficult decision of whether or not to have your pet put to sleep.

Most owners find the decision concerning euthanasia a very difficult one and often seek the advice of the vet. Almost any vet would take the view that the relationship between cat and owner is a two-way contract. You have cared for your cat and made its life as full and satisfying as possible. In return the cat has rewarded you with the pleasure of its company. If the work of nursing your dying pet is proving stressful and starts to have an adverse effect on your health, or if the animal is suffering terribly, then having it put to sleep should be considered. Although vets are qualified to judge when the pain is too great for the cat to bear, they cannot know how you are feeling, or

how your life is being affected. Ultimately it is up to you to decide when the partnership should finish: you will usually know when that time has come.

Holistic care can be of great assistance even at this difficult time. Both you and the cat can benefit from the Bach Flower remedy *Walnut*, which can help to relieve the stress and cope with the change brought about by major life transitions. Homeopathic *Arsen. alb.* given in rising potencies, helps to dispel the fear of dying that the cat may experience towards the end of a long terminal illness. For grief, *Ignatia* is a good remedy for you

△ Your cat should have a long, happy life and a dignified death. Good holistic medicine throughout its life will help it to achieve that end.

to take: it will help the grieving process and allow you to adjust to the loss of your cat. If the grief seems never-ending, *Natrum mur.* can help you finally come to terms with the death of your pet.

▷ The homeopathic remedies ignatia or natrum mur. will help you through the grief that accompanies the loss of a great friend.

◁ The Bach Flower remedy walnut can help both you and your cat during the last few days of its life.

Useful Addresses

UNITED KINGDOM
**Association of British
Veterinary Acupuncture**
East Park Cottage
Handcross
Haywards Heath
West Sussex RH17 6BD

**Association of Chartered
Physiotherapists in Animal
Therapy (ACPAT)**
Morland House
Salters Lane
Winchester
Hampshire SO22 5JP
Tel: (01962) 844 390

The Bach Centre
Mount Vernon
Bakers Lane
Brightwell-cum-Sotwell
Oxfordshire OX10 OPZ
www.bachcentre.com

**British Association of Homeopathic
Veterinary Surgeons (BAHVS)**
The Alternative Veterinary
Medicine Centre
Chinham House
Stanford-in-the-Vale
Oxfordshire SN7 8NQ
www.bahvs.com

**British Holistic Veterinary
Medicine Association (BHVMA)**
The Croft
Tockwith Road
Long Marston
North Yorkshire YO26 7PQ
Tel: (01743) 261 155

**McTimoney Chiropractic
Association (MCA)**
Crowmarsh Gifford
Wallingford
Oxfordshire OX10 8DJ
www.mctimoneychiropractic.org

UNITED STATES
**American Holistic Veterinary
Medical Association (AHVMA)**
PO Box 630
Abingdon, MD 21009-0630
www.ahvma.org

**International Veterinary
Acupuncture Society (IVAS)**
1730 South College Avenue, Suite 301
Fort Collins, CO 80525
www.ivas.org

**International Association for
Veterinary Homeopathy (IAVH)**
Susan G. Wynn, DVM
334 Knollwood Lane
Woodstock, GA 30188
www.iavh.org

**American Veterinary
Chiropractic Association (AVCA)**
442154 E 140 Road
Bluejacket, OK 74333
www.animalchiropractic.org

**Academy of Veterinary
Homeopathy (AVH)**
PO Box 232282
Leucadia, CA 92023-2282
www.theavh.org

CANADA
Canadian Veterinary Medical Association
339 Booth Street
Ottawa
Ontario K1R 7K1
www.canadianveterinarians.net

Ontario Veterinary College
University of Guelph
50 Stone Road
Guelph
Ontario N1G 2W1
www.ovc.uoguelph.ca

AUSTRALIA
Balmain Village Veterinary Clinic
11 Beattie Street
Balmain NSW 2041
www.balmainvillagevet.com.au

Glen Osmond Veterinary Clinic
308 Glen Osmond Road
Fullarton SA 5063
www.glenosmondvet.com.au

Greencross Vets Forest Lake
447 Waterford Road
Ellen Grove QLD 4077
www.greencrossvet.com.au/
Clinic-4/Forest-Lake.aspx

Acknowledgements

The author and publisher would like to
thank the following for their help and
advice in the production of this book:
Anna Brown, Jane Burton, Fiona Doubleday,
Kay McCarroll, Stuart Macgregor, Carolyn
Richards, Catherine Richards, Peter Richards,
Britta Stent and Narelle Stubbs. And not
forgetting… Alexandria, Annie, Asphodel,
Aster, Cobweb, Cosmos, Cleo, Dainty,
Desdemona, Donna, Eyebright, Fat Felix,
Fleur, Gabby, Gemma, Glender, Kitty, Lima,
Lowlander, Mandy, Mussy, Noname, Oosha,
Ozzie, Pearl, Peony, Primrose, Sabrina, Sinatra,
Snowy, Tagor, Tallulah, Tigger and Zorro.

Index

abdomen 80–1
acupuncture 32, 52–3
aggression 66–7
allergies 83
aromatherapy 32, 48–9
arthritis 89
artificial respiration 92
asthma 79
aural haematoma 75
Ayurvedic medicine 32, 46, 58

Bach flowers 32, 56–7, 62, 64–5
birth 28–9
bites 75, 85, 88, 93
bladder 81
bleeding 92
bones 88–9
breeding cats 28–9
brushing 22–3
burns 93

cancer 51, 74, 90–1
cat flaps 16–17
cataracts 73
catteries 14, 25, 65, 68
chest 78–9
Chinese medicine 32, 46, 52
chiropractic 32, 40–1
chlamydia 25
climbing frames 20
conjunctivitis 71–2
contraception 26–7
convulsions 87
corneal ulcers 72–3
cost of cat ownership 14, 28
coughs 78–9
crystal therapies 32, 58–9, 62

destructiveness 69
diarrhoea 80–1
dietary requirements 18–19
discharges 70, 71, 74–5, 84

ears 22, 74–5
emotional health 8, 10, 11, 32
energy systems 8, 32, 58
enteritis 25
euthanasia 94
exercising your cat 20
eyes 22, 71–3

feeding your cat 18–19
female system 84
first aid treatments 92–3

glaucoma 72–3
grief 94
grooming 22–3

health in cats 10
herbalism 32, 46–7, 64, 66
holistic therapies 8, 11, 32–3, 62
homeopathy 32, 54–5, 62
hormone system 86
house-training 21, 64–5
housing your cat 16–17
hunting 20

inflammation 71
influenza 25
injuries 23, 88, 92–3

jealousy 70

kidneys 81
Kirlian photography 8
kittens 10, 20, 28–9, 67
    house-training 21
    vaccinations 25

leukaemia (FeLV) 25, 27, 28
litter trays 21
liver 81
locomotor system 88–9
lungs 78–9

male tract 85
massage 32, 34–5
microchipping 14
middle and inner ear infections 75
mouth 22, 77

neoplasia 90–1
nervous system 87
neuralgia 87
neutering 26–7
nose 22, 76

osteopathy 32, 38–9
outdoor runs 17

pain relief 78, 79, 85, 88
pancreas 81
parasites 24, 74, 80, 82–3
pharmaceuticals 50–1
physiotherapy 32, 36–7
pining 68
poisoning 87, 93
pregnancy 28–9

rabies 14
Reiki 44–5, 62
reproduction 26–7, 28–9
rheumatism 89
roundworms 24

scalds 93
scratching posts 69
skin 68, 82–3
sterilization 26–7
stings 93

TTouch 42–3, 62
tapeworms 24
teeth 22, 77
throat 77
toys 20
tumours 76, 77, 86, 87, 89

vaccinations 14, 25
veterinary practice
    8, 10, 11, 50–1, 62
vitamin supplements
    19, 89
vomiting 80–1

water 19
worming your
    cat 24
wounds 23,
    92–3

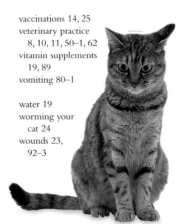